HELLO BLOCKCHAIN

Lao Jiadi

Prunus Press USA

Original Title:《你好啊，区块链》
Original book by Orient Publishing Center

This edition is published by arrangement with Prunus Press USA, through the agency of China National Publications Import and Export (Group) Co., Ltd.

HELLO BLOCKCHAIN

Written by Lao Jiadi
Translated by Haiwang Yuan
Designed by Wu Yanfeng & Brandy Ding

First Edition 2023
ISBN: 978-1-61612-158-7

本书获得上海翻译出版促进计划支持

Prunus Press USA

Foreword

Blockchain Has Always Been a Serious Technology

Liu Xingliang

I published my *Blockchain in China* in early 2019, when people knew little about blockchain and even had a negative view. Therefore, its publication was under a lot of pressure.

In 2017, China stopped the issuance of ICO and cracked down on the illegal practice of accumulating wealth through financing under the pretext of blockchain. Simultaneously, it was also planning for the CBDC (Central Bank Digital Currency) and steadily promoting the application of blockchain to finance, medicine, and education. Many people fail to see the big trend due to their misunderstanding of blockchain.

China officially recognized the technological status of blockchain on October 24, 2019. I was overjoyed! I was happy not only because my book would be a hit but also because the name of blockchain was finally rectified after undergoing hardships and negative "treatment." We now have correct guidance.

Right then, I truly felt that blockchain had become a hit throughout China overnight. Soon after, various people pestered me for interviews, book manuscripts, and lectures because they knew I had been researching blockchain early on.

Whether producing media programs, giving interviews, or writing articles and books, I try my best to explain blockchain in an easy-to-understand manner to avoid confusing the reader or audience. However, blockchain can't be interpreted with such banal examples as "accounts of the expenses of dating can be kept with blockchain technology" or "mining cryptocurrency is like playing mahjong." The reason is that the technology is built on underlying technologies such as cryptography. One must do a lot of thinking before thoroughly understanding its architectural principles and even understanding its application scenarios and future directions.

Being a writer has been my dream. The urge to share and the desire to achieve the matching ability have always driven me to move forward toward the goal. I have tried hard to interpret enigmatic science and technology romantically and stylishly. So, when I saw that a dodo, resurrected with revived genes, was trying to use the perspective of a future prophet to show everyone the charm of blockchain, I couldn't help clapping and shouting that it was intriguing.

Let me give you three tips on embarking on the thinking trip following the book *Hello Blockchain!*

First, think as you read it.

Although there are 99 separate entries in the book, if you only want to embellish your language with one or two of them when you chat with others, you'll blaspheme the book's ingenuity. After all, few people can explain the concepts of "public blockchain," "private blockchain," "consortium blockchain," "hash function," "SHA-256," "homomorphic hashing," "symmetrical encryption," asymmetric encryption," "digital signature," "blind signature," "ring signature," and "multi-signature" naturally with simple examples. These concepts are the basis for understanding blockchain and its initial application form, bitcoin. It isn't enough only to browse around the operation mechanism, internal structure, external interests, and the history and presence of blockchain. It is recommended that you read from the front to the back before reading it in chapters and then eventually read it with the illustrations. When you get the logic of all the concepts, you'll more than understand blockchain.

Second, think about and reflect on it.

I have said that I started working on the Internet early and always ponder and reflect on the future of technology and human choice at the technological crossroad. However, it seems challenging for a thick and enigmatic popular science book to express all my reflections. As for the future of technology, the world, and humanity, whose viewpoints are they? Are they objective and credible? Or we may as well give up commenting and only lay bare the facts, leading the judgment to the reader. The book *Hello Blockchain!* manages to explain abstruse technology in a light and intriguing way. It is also straightforward. For example, it claims, "Technology itself isn't a sin." Its courage may be commendable, but opinions differ over whether the comment is appropriate.

Third, the chain is limitless.

Can blockchain be explained away with mere 99 entries? The answer is a definite no. After all, how can blockchain based on complex technology be used in daily life, and how can it be operated to build a decentralized environment? These are indeed tough questions to answer. By saying so, I mean blockchain development is still at an early stage. But it promises a bright future.

But now, I suggest not giving up the opportunity to enter the blockchain world. Come on, let's follow Mr. Dodo's steps!

Introduction

When I first met with Mr. Dodo, I was standing by the fountain near the Hoover Tower on the campus of Standford University, trying to interview the professors and students passing by. Sticking my microphone to them, I asked, "Hi, do you want to know about blockchain?" The flowers around were ablaze with various colors, but I felt frustrated with the "no" answers.

That was a summer day in 2017 when I went to San Francisco for a fintech summit. A group of "crazy people" who wanted to change the world tried to persuade the entire Silicon Valley to put together a seven-piece puzzle in a decentralized manner. However, I was dealt a cruel blow when I stepped out of the enthusiastic conference room because public and industry insiders' cognition of blockchain was split entirely.

Oh, humans who crave new knowledge only want to befriend blockchain casually in their piecemeal spare time. Simultaneously, such concepts, more frigid and abstruse than computer code, as mining, hash algorithm, double-spending, and stablecoin are looming large. How can we dissect them and make them appealing to industry outsiders so they can savor them with milk-form toppings and favorite snacks like spicy bars?

"Hi! Hello!" A feeble voice came from behind the fountain sprays. The sight was like the image viewed through a gigantic prism. As I looked closely, I saw a tiny figure with a bird's head and a curved beak standing on the staircase with a red cloak thrown on his back. How I wished I could instantly change myself into the "Redeemer!" It was an inch-tall elf that the omnipotent Monkey King had transformed himself and hid in the treasure casket held in the hands of his master, the Tang Monk, depicted in the famed Chinese classic fantasy novel *Journey to the West*.

That was my first encounter with Mr. Dodo. This little guy wasn't part of the diet for the 16th-century colonists, but a new species brought back to life with his genes resurrected who had traveled back from the near future. With a decision made on the spur of the moment, I pocketed the little guy with all the world's secret files in his brain and brought him back to Shanghai.

It was Mr. Dodo who accompanied me as I finished this book. In North China, where the winter is so damp that people from North China can never understand, I even put a felt hat and a down-filled coat on him. Sitting on a pile of books, he told me what would happen in the near future.

He was a wandering guitarist. He could get paid with digital currency whenever someone requested a piece of music from him so that he could exchange for his provisions with it from the intelligent farm: the dodo tree (Sideroxylon grandiflorum) seeds. He liked the dodo tree seeds because the product could be tracked from processing to storage, and he never had to worry about eating bad seeds sold by dishonest growers. He also claimed that no ID was required for this fantastic time-traveling since everything was registered on the blockchain.

"What are you here for?" I asked, unable to suppress the curiosity that suddenly hit upon me.

The moon was brilliant, and Mr. Dodo was sleeping in my arms. Indeed, years after being swept by the tide of the Internet, our world has been covered with dust again. A promising entrepreneur who still munched a hamburger on a bicycle years ago has turned into a "moneyed man" who has benefited from this rule of the game today.

You, who have gotten used to online ride-hailing services, may find it hard to imagine how to make a trip without a go-between platform. As a smartphone owner, you may have never thought of getting free from the current financial payment system. Perhaps, the world can be reorganized more efficiently and less costly one day, and this possibility is simply fascinating.

To answer the call coming from my inner self, I left the traditional journalist circle a decade ago. With my pen and comprehension, I started a career of paying tribute to the "feasible world" in the near future. "I want to write a popular science book readable and appealing to even a technical novice. I want him to look at the possibilities in a relaxed manner." I said that to Mr. Dodo and my image in the mirror. He took off his red cloak and handed it to me.

It took me a long time to write this book. Although I learned about blockchain many years ago due to the nature of my work, I still found it challenging to explain so much of the nitty-gritty of the technology in vivid and accurate terms. It was more difficult considering the philosophical thinking about blockchain I put together in this book.

I thank the three technological consultants whose support kept me away from loneliness.

I'm also thankful to Mr. Dodo, whose existence has convinced me that technology can make the world in the near future more flexible and warmer. Such confidence gives humans, insignificant as they are, their pride.

One midnight, I stuck my head out of my tent and saw fiery-red lava bursting out of the earth's crest at the mouth of Mount Nyiragongo and churning ceaselessly. I knew it was the pulse of this blue planet, the beautiful globe always bringing forth new things. Finally, I am dedicating this book to my loved one. I have always believed you can also give birth to a new world.

Lao Jiadi

From Shanghai, China, on March 23, 2020

Contents

PART

1

Basic Terms

01 Blockchain

Business transactions occurred in antiquity when people traded stone axes with goat skin. People involved in the exchanges often used various authenticating symbols to trust each other. For example, a tribal chief of noble character and high prestige or a cold commercial bank has played the roles of witnesses and bookkeepers of the transactions In the long history of humanity.

The emergence of blockchain technology means that we have entered the era of endorsing our business transactions with nothing but codes.

Like iron chains and gold necklaces, blockchain, as its name demonstrates, is also a series of connected rings, except that they are abstract blocks instead of iron or pearl rings. Their functions may have extended later, but they initially worked on recording the information of every transaction.

We can treat blockchain as a perfect ledger keeping transaction vouchers. Tribal chiefs are bribable and likely to disown a debt after receiving bribers' precious shells. But there is no way for blockchains to cheat because the price for falsifying this blockchain ledger is too high.

Interlocked "chains" connect all the data recorded in the blockchain.

You may have placed the "ice-breaking" game at a new-arrival-welcoming meeting on a university campus. A teacher invites the first student to give a two-minute self-introduction on "hobbies." The teacher then asks another student to introduce himself while simplifying the previous student's self-introduction into "name plus hobbies" and recounting it. A third student will do what the second student does.

In the gigantic blockchain ledger, each block is a page of the account book, which is likened to a student mentioned above. The beginning of the second page records the vital information of the first page. The beginning of the third page contains the essential part of the second page, and so on. Each page preserves the vital information of the previous page.

Then, an ill-intentioned person who wants to tamper with one of the pages must doctor each of the following pages.

It is like a spring tour organized in a kindergarten. The children file forward, and a teacher asks each to remember the child in front of them. The teacher will call the roll when the children gather after the trip. If one student tells the wrong name, it proves that not all the children are back and that the file isn't in its original order.

The hacker's tragedy doesn't end there. The blockchain ledger isn't in the hands of a government or a financial magnate. Instead, it has unlimited "copies" distributed to all the people in the blockchain for them to keep.

Some people who like to contribute their storage hard drives keep a giant ledger, and most are geeks advocating network stability and big shots that can benefit from the blockchain network. Others take care of the remaining parts of the account book.

As the account book's keepers are highly dispersed, hackers must falsify all the "copies" of the ledger kept by everyone before they can achieve their aim. The result would be the same even if they smashed one of the ledge-keeping servers. It is like the case of a QR code that can still be readable even if you blot out one of the tiny blocks. Since the "copies" of the ledger contain repetitive information, the destruction of some of them would also come to naught.

It is blockchain's nature to increase the cost of falsification with technology and guarantee the data's credibility. This nature has quickly enabled it to extend from business transactions to more profound and broader areas. Blockchain is no longer only responsible for transaction bookkeeping. It has penetrated all fields where safety for data storage is needed, thus becoming a super database that is difficult to falsify.

Whenever we look back on the development of blockchain technology, the most exciting thing is that, for the first time, human beings have been liberated from the outdated thinking that they must rely on one person or institution to achieve mutual trust. From this perspective, blockchain is a fantastic trend of thought.

02 Decentralization

If centralization is totalitarian, decentralization can be understood as the separation of powers. In other words, there won't be a center to have the final say.

Where the Internet is concerned, webpages and portals are centralized as they are of the "you-listen-to-what-I-say" broadcasting model. On the contrary, We Media is decentralized because of its "everyone-is-a-broadcaster" model.

You can also find some scenarios of decentralization. If you study a course on an online teaching platform, you will come into contact with the "peer-review" mode of examinations.

In the past, only teachers corrected their students' papers, and they alone had the final word on what grades you would get and whether you could pass and graduate.

However, with the "peer-review" mechanism, the teacher doesn't monopolize the right to grade. The system would randomly distribute the class assignment papers to you and three more students studying the same course as you. And completing the grading is a prerequisite for getting your exam score.

Each grade has the same weight, and it doesn't matter if you are a popular student. Under this decentralized scoring mechanism, you can not only obtain a relatively fair score but also enjoy a complete sense of participation in decision-making.

That is the beauty of decentralization.

Then, why is the blockchain decentralized?

Blockchain also has the advantage of peer review, and this database is under no one's or institution's control. It is like the teacher is no longer the grader who can decide his students' fate.

Anyone, if he will, can become a decision-maker in a blockchain. It's like you have the right to give a score of "0" to a nonsense-making paper. Someone's departure wouldn't cause the blockchain to collapse. It is like the situation where one of your fellow students suddenly quits reading your exam paper and wouldn't affect the scoring at large. Your paper would be automatically allotted to another fellow student. The consequence of leaving the "peer-review" process would only result in the quitter's failure to pass this course's exam.

This decentralized feature of blockchain completely subverts the current concept of business transactions. In the real world today, any of your monetary transactions with anyone must be done in a centralized mode: a bank or a third payment party must record the information of your transactions on their ledger. Only through this third party can your transactions be guaranteed to occur.

On a blockchain, however, the transaction information is added to the ledger via each interloping chain-like page, and each one on the chain keeps a copy of the ledger to witness the transactions together. Therefore, you don't have to worry about your account being falsified because the transactions are even more decentralized. For that matter, the application of blockchain technology to data storage is also a victory of decentralization.

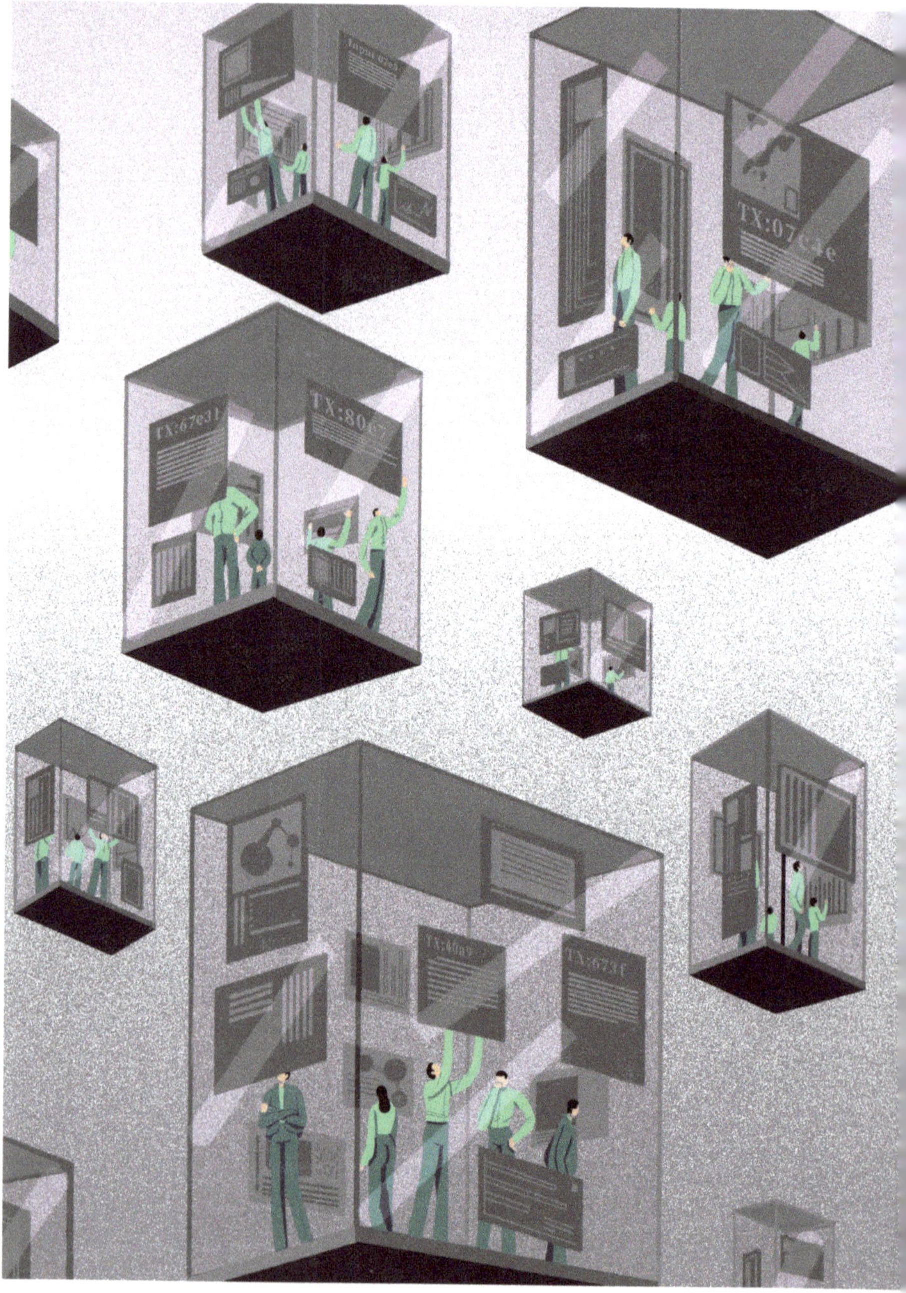
TX:67e31

03 Private Blockchain

A private blockchain is built by a single company and belongs to it internally. What is recorded on the chain is the information about the company's own affairs.

Now, you need to learn something about how the information service works in a traditional enterprise. Only then can you understand what a private blockchain means. Enterprise information systems generally reduce the risk of malicious data modification through permission control and then monitor the system behavior of each permission role through the security log.

Specifically, the technical staff within the enterprise doesn't have the authority to modify or delete a business record. Although the supervisor of a business department has the power to alter the data, each of his modification behavior is recorded in the system's security log without exception. In this way, when conducting an information security audit, a company can detect that supervisor's suspicious actions that violate the chain of command.

Such a system looks pretty secure, but what if the security log is modified? What if influential people with authority to alter the record wanted to do evil?

Now, it is time for the private blockchain to play its role. Companies can build a private blockchain to record all its information in every block.

Suppose you are currently trying to woo a pretty girl and plan to observe what she is doing in secret. One day, you sneak into her diary in cyberspace and inevitably leave a "footprint." It worries you so much that you can't eat and sleep well. Suddenly, you hit upon an idea: *Can I ask my techy buddy to clean up my "footprint" in her cyberspace diary?*

Any "incursion" would leave a trace in the traditional database, and this techy buddy can satisfy your request if he has the authority to delete the "footprint" you've left. What would happen if the company had established a private blockchain?

Since everyone's footprints are recorded in the blocks linked together, the techy buddy who wants to delete one of the "footprints" must not only modify all the blocks after the one with the print but also modify the block ledger kept by everyone else. Naturally, he must give up the idea that seems a fantasy.

Another method is to secretly turn off the function of recording footprints when the system is updated, but your buddy doesn't want to risk being fired by the company. He found that unless he is able enough to replace the original code, the existence of the private blockchain determines that he can only complete the mission by adding a piece of information stating that you haven't stepped on diary cyberspace in a new block.

To save face in your presence, he happily made a decision.

Eventually, you will be embarrassed to find on your computer that you have left two footprints simultaneously in the girl's cyberspace: "X (your name) has left his footprint," and "X (your name) hasn't left his footprint."

The existence of the private blockchain makes any falsifying attempt more challenging. Perhaps, you may have discovered that the ledger in the private blockchain may be in the hands of different people from the same institution abiding by the same rules of the game. They may have reached an agreement of shared interests in real life. Therefore, private blockchains aren't entirely decentralized.

04 Consortium Blockchain

The consortium blockchain has more than one participant compared to the private blockchain. Therefore, due to the participation of different subjects, a check and balance of interests is formed.

First of all, what is a consortium? It is reflected in the movie *Once Upon a Time in America*. A group of young loafers put the money they have earned through their mafia transactions into a leather briefcase, lock it in a safe deposit box in a train station, and give the key to a friend outside their gang. They agree that the friend can hand over the key only when all the loafer brothers are on the spot.

It is a simple example of a consortium.

Of course, the business situation of the consortium blockchain is much more complicated than this relationship. You can imagine such a scenario: You often buy bread in a chain bakery and accumulate many points, and a chain milk tea shop next to you has an idea: *Can we use the two stores' points interchangeably?*

This way, after accumulating a certain number of points from the bakery, a consumer can also go to the milk tea shop for a discount. It sounds like a good idea to boost consumption, but a problem arises immediately.

Suppose, in a short time, the number of consumers of the milk tea shop drops with each passing day while the bakery's business thrives increasingly. The jealous owner of the milk tea shop, who wants to cripple the bakery's business, then forges a large amount of non-existent transaction records so that more people can exchange their points for discounted bread at the bakery.

Although the milk tea shop also needs to give discounts to these consumers who have accumulated many points, its loss is minimum due to the poor consumer flow. But it can cause more economic losses to the bakery enjoying a heavy customer flow.

So, how can we build the underlying trust? At this point, the consortium blockchain provides a possible remedy.

They build a "point-accumulation chain" together, and each transaction record of a loaf of bread or a cup of milk tea is written into blocks and stored on the chain. A conflict with the bakery's ledger will instantly foil the milk tea shop's conspiracy when the milk tea shop wants to modify the account book and write transactions that don't exist because the transaction ledger is shared by the milk tea shop and the bakery.

In real life, consortium blockchains are also used in more complex business scenarios, where participants in the consortium make their decisions on the number of participants, the rules they each must follow, and the increase or decrease in the number of participants. Like the milk tea shop and bakery, the consortium blockchain makes it easier for these participants to trust each other. However, as far as the public is concerned, the consortium blockchain isn't entirely decentralized since it is under these participants' control. In many consortium blockchains, the permissions of various participants are also different, so each participant may not have an equal voice.

05 Public Blockchain

The public blockchain is entirely decentralized, not controlled by any company or consortium of financial magnates. A large number of anonymous public participants jointly maintain the operation of the chain.

Here is a specific example: There is now a singing talent contest, and there are three judging methods:

1. An organizer forms an internal panel of judges;
2. Stakeholders, sponsors, and other cooperative institutions form a joint committee of judges;
3. SMS is used for voting in the finals, and the judges became the public participants whose backgrounds and identities can never be known.

These three review methods can be compared to the relationship between private, consortium, and public blockchains.

There is no doubt that bitcoin is the most well-known public blockchain in the world today. But the operation of this public blockchain has long been verified and practiced in a very ancient and savage way.

Micronesia is now a central Pacific archipelago that anthropologists pay more attention to, and it has a magical isle called Yap. Since their ancestors conquered the Pacific Ocean with canoes, the islanders have almost been

isolated from the rest of the world. The 5,000-6,000 islanders in various villages used a decentralized mechanism of currency circulation in the early 20th century.

The "currency" used by the islanders consisted of doughnut-like rocks, some too large to carry during daily transactions. During each business dealing, the two trading islanders announced it in front of the boulder. Their fellow villagers came to testify to the transaction. The two parties also invited the chief of the entire island and the respected elders from each village to witness the business activity. Those massive stones weren't actually moved, but since every witness at the scene recorded the moment in their memory, the deal thus went into effect.

The death of an elder of his old age wouldn't affect the result of the transaction record. Suppose one party wanted to collude with the witnesses to deny it unilaterally. In that case, it would almost be impossible for them to succeed because they couldn't tamper with the transaction memory in other people's minds at the same time.

This trading circle witnessed and recorded by the public is similar to a public blockchain. You can think of the chief and the elders as the keepers of the entire account book. They witnessed every transaction with their presence in various villages on the island. Meanwhile, the residents of each village kept part of the transaction's ledger, which generally recorded the business deals happening among their fellow villagers.

Quarrying the "doughnut-like" stones was costly, and their reserve was limited. The Yap islanders might not keep their money in their bank account like modern people, but they could show how wealthy they were with various numbers and sizes of the stones in their possession.

Interestingly, there was also a wealthy man on the island whose stone no one had seen. But the chief and the villagers remembered that his ancestors had quarried a massive "doughnut." Unfortunately, their boat had capsized while they tried to ship it, leaving the stone lying at the bottom of the vast Pacific Ocean.

This "shared memory" was the basis for the existence of the "stone coins." The ecology of the public blockchain also depends on the consensus of every participant.

Yap Island has now switched to US dollars due to the influx of modern civilization to cope with the more frequent commodity transactions. Those stones covered with moss are quietly stacked in the backyard or squares for tourists to view.

However, we, who have been using modern currencies such as RMB and US dollars, chose to follow their ideas and created a public blockchain like Bitcoin. We can only see this phenomenon as a miraculous example of historical reincarnation.

06 Bitcoin

There isn't a single coin or banknote in the world that has the value of Bitcoin inscribed on it. In a superficial sense, this is because Bitcoin is a cryptocurrency and hasn't been given an entity. In a more profound sense, it is because the coins and banknotes circulating in the real world are all minted and issued by the central bank of a specific country. On the contrary, Bitcoin has broken free from such a currency logic because no government or financial magnate controls it. Therefore, it has the attributes of complete decentralization.

Decentralization means that there is no central monetary system behind Bitcoin. The banking system endorses transactions in traditional currencies as the state regulates the total amount of money circulating in the market.

Suppose you want to transfer one yuan to another person. Despite your relationship with the other party, you have no need to worry about him denying the transaction because your transfer request has been sent to the bank for the record.

Suppose you want to deal face-to-face with the other party. It would be best to use common sense to identify the authenticity of the banknotes. Common sense comes from a series of anti-counterfeiting details published by the banknote printing plant.

The money printing machine's switch is in the state's hands. In most cases, you don't have to worry that one day an unidentified person flips the switch and prints a lot of banknotes to inflate the value of the money in your pocket overnight.

Do you see it? The smooth operation of the central monetary system depends on "trust." The system works because you trust the bank and the state.

A state's or bank's authoritative symbol disappears in the new Bitcoin system. The entire Bitcoin ecosystem is built on blockchain technology, which guarantees the fairness and trustworthiness of the underlying operating rules.

Now, let's see how it works.

First, there is no bitcoin-minting machine in the world. The creator created a supply cap of 21 million bitcoins the day it was born. You can simply compare it to the rules of the game written into the programming code from the very beginning.

The rate of bitcoin production is also pre-set, and the number will have reached the 21 million cap by about 2140. Just like gold and oil reserves on the earth are constant, bitcoins can only be mined slowly, and no one has the right to overproduce them.

Second, all bitcoin transactions don't need to go through a central settlement system, and each coin transaction is recorded based on blockchain technology.

As mentioned earlier, blockchain technology means that each transaction is recorded in a block. Suppose a blockchain can be called an enormous ledger. In that case, since each page of information in the ledger is closely related to the information on the next page, you don't have to worry about someone maliciously tampering with a data page to cheat.

The copy of the ledger is multiplied and distributed to all the people on the blockchain. Then, they can keep it together. Unlike traditional currency, the account book is kept in the bank's database.

In addition, the bookkeeper isn't an authority you must accept, and everyone on the chain, including you, has the right to compete to become the bookkeeper.

With these technical features, the trusting relationship that the state or bank initially needs to build has been established to allow every bitcoin transaction to be carried out directly.

In today's world, the vast majority of countries don't recognize Bitcoin's currency status but tend to define it as a virtual commodity.

However, Bitcoin fans believe that if we look back on our history, currency was formed based on the consensus of a group and a region. Before knowing the concepts of state and bank, humans spontaneously used shells or stones to buy cows and sheep.

Perhaps, the embryonic form of the currency may show that it is nothing but a collective imagination. As long as a consensus is formed, anything can be used as currency.

They regard Bitcoin's birth as a brilliant moment in the history of money because of the reduction of the currency's essence.

- **Related vocabulary**

  19. Fiat currency
  20. Cryptocurrency and digital currency

07 Satoshi Nakamoto

Satoshi Nakamoto is the creator of Bitcoin.

In November 2008, he proposed the concept of Bitcoin in a covert cryptography discussion group. In his report at the time, "Bitcoin: A Peer-to-Peer Electronic Cash System," he provided a brief but nuanced sketch of how the Bitcoin world worked.

Subsequently, he devoted himself to developing bitcoin issuance, transaction, and account management systems and dug out the first block on January 4, 2009, Beijing time.

After that, his whereabouts became highly mysterious.

Though he never showed up, he is well-received by cryptocurrency enthusiasts worldwide as the Father of Bitcoin. Countless people were inspired by his report at the time because it opened the door to the paradise of currency.

Although he used the name Satoshi Nakamoto and stated in an online profile that he lived in Japan, the email address he used to communicate with the outside world came from a free service center in Germany, which adds a suspenseful tint to his identity.

Various reporters searched high and low throughout the world for the physical him. They even hid in the trash cans downstairs of several "suspects'" residences, lying in wait to catch sight of this technical geek who dared to challenge the authority of currency.

Yet all came to nothing. The Internet, which can quickly "human flesh search" anyone's identity, has covered it for several years. And now, it seems to be able to do so for a long time.

We can write a brief biography of Satoshi Nakamoto in a few words because he has gradually faded out of the Internet and has never aired his views on Bitcoin since December 2010. Legend has it that until the end of April 2011, he only emailed a few core Bitcoin developers before completely cutting off his contact with the outside world.

As bitcoins have gradually entered the homes of ordinary people from the niche of the geek circles, people still have no way of knowing the true identity of Satoshi Nakamoto. Although several self-claimed Satoshi Nakamotos have surfaced, they were all discovered to be imposters. The claim that he committed suicide has never been substantiated, either.

The story of Satoshi Nakamoto later evolved into conspiracy theories. Some suspected he wasn't a single person. Instead, he was the incarnation of four companies: Samsung, Toshiba, Nakamichi, and Motorola, as his name might be abbreviated from them. Others suspected that it was an

indescribable mysterious organization.

But the gossip has never prevented Satoshi Nakamoto's ardent fans from worshiping him.

In 2015, UCLA's finance professor Bhagwan Chowdhry said he had nominated Satoshi Nakamoto as a candidate for the 2016 Nobel Prize in Economics.

Raving about him, he said, "I am serious about recommending Satoshi Nakamoto to be the award recipient. The invention of Bitcoin, in particular, and cryptocurrency, in general, can be said to be revolutionary."

Of course, there is no precedent for the Nobel Prize to be awarded to anonymous people. But Satoshi Nakamoto's contribution to humanity is indeed remarkable. People have been fantasizing about building a lower-cost transaction network in the traditional environment. However, building complete trust among strangers without going through a centralized institution with strong endorsing power, such as banks, account settlement centers, and brokerages, has always been challenging.

Satoshi Nakamoto's primary contribution is designing a set of bitcoin issuance mechanisms, which not only technically ensures the foundation of trust in network transactions but, more importantly, subverts the stereotyped human perception of currency. His successors have refined his technical achievements in these mechanisms into the "blockchain."

The date of birth that Satoshi Nakamoto has provided on the Internet is April 5, 1975, which is pretty meaningful.

On the same day in 1933, US President Franklin Roosevelt issued the famous Executive Order No. 6102, declaring that private hoarding of gold was illegal in the United States. It forced the public to sell their gold to the Federal Reserve. Subsequently, the US government devalued the dollar by 40% to combat the Great Depression running rampant at that time.

Listing his birthday as this day, Satoshi Nakamoto may have meant to make an ironic statement against the abuse of currency power. It is generally believed that, by choosing a time of a steep economic crisis to create Bitcoin, Satoshi Nakamoto wanted to build a utopian society in which the power of currency is returned to the hands of ordinary people.

His fall off of the face of the earth is undoubtedly the best footnote to this original intention of his.

08 Genesis Block

The genesis block was mined by Satoshi Nakamoto, the Father of Bitcoin.

What is the concept of "mining?" It is commonly understood as similar to coal mining, except that it "mines" the answer to a puzzle through computer operations, unlike the dust-covered coal miner who must wield a shovel in a mine shaft.

Every time a new block is mined, bitcoins are rewarded. The genesis block's reward is 50 bitcoins, naturally put under Satoshi Nakamoto's name.

But it is worth mentioning that these 50 bitcoins are unusable. Opinions differ on whether it was Satoshi Nakamoto's intent or negligence when he

The Times an/2009 Chancellor on the brink of second bailout for banks.

coded the program.

The only thing that can be determined is why it can't be used: The transaction record that Satoshi Nakamoto obtained 50 bitcoins isn't written into the blockchain transaction database. When bitcoins are transferred, coins that can't be traced back to the source can never be used. In other words, the 50 bitcoins are illegal from the perspective of the transaction process.

The situation is equivalent to someone claiming that he gave someone else a gold coin, but no one believes that he ever owned it. Even if he later claims to give someone else the gold coin, the alleged transaction won't be recognized.

In the parameters of this transaction record, Satoshi Nakamoto also meaningfully wrote down the headline of the article on the front page of *The Times* that day, "*The Times*: 30/Jan/2009 Chancellor on the brink of a second bailout for banks."

This sentence can pin the time of blockchain's creation on the hours after the newspaper issue's publication. It can be seen from the original text of this report that the UK was mired in a swamp of bad credit at that time, and its banks systemic risks devastated the Central Bank and the Chancellor of Finance.

It is also intriguing why Satoshi Nakamoto chose the title of this article. Bitcoin was born against the backdrop of the global financial crisis, which began with the collapse of Lehman Brothers in 2008, the same year that Satoshi Nakamoto released Bitcoin's "White Paper."

Some believe he was determined to create Bitcoin because he worried about the problems arising from the existing centralized financial system.

09 Blocks

With pieces of data stored in it, a block is the basic blockchain unit. If you think of a blockchain as a dream empire built out of Lego bricks, its blocks are like superimposed plastic building bricks. There are studs on each Lego brick's surface used to connect with the next brick. Each block

40a9e
TX:80e7f

has a similar design known as the block header containing the "getHeader message." It is written at the top of each block's header packet.

The information stored in the block header occupies only a tiny part of the space. Take Bitcoin as an example. The fixed size of each block is some megabytes. In contrast, the block header takes only 80 bytes. But this "small stud" records the summary of various information from the previous block header and outlines the information in this area. Therefore, block headers string the blocks together like a chain.

You may feel free to think of the block header as the opening summary of an episode of a TV series. For example, in the American TV series Supernatural, the previous episode's synopsis and the current episode's highlights are shown before the feature. A block is like an episode's feature, with the block header combining the previous episode's synopsis and the current episode's highlights.

A block differs from a TV series episode in that the former has the next episode's preview at the end, but a block doesn't contain the information of the next one.

Suppose an enthusiast wants to edit a TV series, condensing 15 seasons of content into a fast-forwarded video clip. He can put together the previous episode's synopsis and the current episode's highlights.

He doesn't have to take the trouble of going through all the feature parts of the episodes if he wants to find out which episode in which a particular plot appears. He can quickly locate it by viewing the synopsis of each episode. Although he can't search for the specific information in a block from its header, he can still instantly verify if a particular piece of data is included.

When he intends to change the content of an episode, he will find it impossible to deceive the audience because the essence of the plot of each episode has been recorded in the previous episode's synopsis at the beginning of the following episode. That is how blockchain actually works.

10 P2P

P2P is short for Peer-to-peer, and the word "peer" means "partner." P2P is translated into "*Dian-dui-dian* (Point-to-Point) in Chinese, and Chinese academic circles refer to P2P as "*Duideng wangluo* (Reciprocal Network)."

The significance of P2P is that each network doesn't have a hierarchy of nodes. They are providers and acquirers of resources simultaneously, with the resources shared without a central node's coordination.

A pure P2P network should be a freely organized network with a high tolerance for the joining and leaving of its nodes. It thus eliminates the need for a central server to exist.

At present, P2P technology is widely used in file sharing. But sometimes, the central node's intervention can't be avoided in these real-world applications.

For example, some software-downloading membership systems prioritize uploading and downloading speed to paying users. This practice has been criticized for destroying the P2P's total autonomy and equality spirit.

Wealth management platforms borrow the concept of P2P, and lending platforms also claim to be P2P platforms. However, these products themselves don't use P2P technology at all.

The network based on the underlying blockchain technology is a pure P2P network.

Let me illustrate P2P with a fictional story. Only a single mini-workshop prints and distributes books on an islet. At first, all the books the tiny islanders read came from the workshop, and they slowly found that some popular books, such as *The Little Prince,* were in short supply.

Then, a tiny wise man came up with a method: Everyone who wants to read *The Little Prince* doesn't have to go to the workshop to wait in line to purchase it. Instead, they can obtain the right to copy some book pages from other book-owning islanders.

The wise man has copied *The Little Prince*'s first 30 pages from a neighbor in the east of the islet and the last 17 pages from a neighbor in the west. Initially, his neighbors were happy to read and distribute copies of the book.

The islanders have solved the resource shortage problem by being readers and distributors simultaneously without the intervention of the workshop. Of course, the concept of copyright is absent on this islet, far away from industrial civilization.

But the story just began. The wise man quickly discovered a problem: In the long run, he needed to give the islanders sufficient incentives to encourage them to copy and distribute popular books willingly. So, he proposed that each could get a small jar of honey for their fellow islanders for every ten pages he shared.

Another problem arose: Such a rule of incentives wasn't enough to discourage dishonest people from withholding their honey after obtaining their shared book pages.

The wise man hit upon a new idea: The islanders share their book pages weekly at the market. Everyone on the scene records the behavior of sharing book pages for honey, thus turning them into witnesses to the transaction.

Oh, these fictitious tiny islanders! They were unaware that their business model would become blockchain-based P2P technology in our Internet-accessible world.

11 Distributed System

When we discuss distributed systems, we are talking about architecting a computer system model. A computer system is said to be distributed if the individual computers work together to accomplish a single task while looking like a single computer from an external perspective.

You might ask why a distributed system is used. After all, managing a system is far more troublesome than working with a single computer. You can imagine yourself as an entrepreneur. Although the difficulty and cost of management are minimized when you are the only one in your company, your maximum "performance" is limited by your talent and diligence.

Suppose you recruit talents specializing in different fields to perform their own duties. In that case, the problem facing you now is no longer a performance bottleneck but how to ensure the effective connection of various links and cooperation of this company.

Let's return to the context of a distributed computing system. A system administrator is to ensure that every computer in the system communicates with each other promptly.

Distributed systems have another huge advantage. Since each computer in the system completes its work independently without interfering with each other, any error occurring in a single computer won't affect the operations of other computers.

Blockchain is a perfect illustration of a large-scale distributed system. Its wisdom lies in that the participants are made up of computers spread around the globe. The same transaction ledger runs and is maintained simultaneously on each participant's computer. It is equivalent to as many "copies" of the account book as participants on a blockchain.

The common goal of these computers, or participants, is to record transactions that each other agrees upon and to maintain the ledger's integrity. The joining or withdrawal of any single participant won't affect the regular operation of the entire blockchain network. That is because as long as there are enough copies of the ledger in the network, the blockchain ecology has sufficient tolerance for individuals' departure.

Interestingly, though all the participants are doing the same thing, they don't need a unified clock because they can follow their time zone precisely as they do in real life. The reason is that another prominent feature

of distributed systems is that each computer works at different times, and administrators aren't willing and able to order them to do something synchronously at a certain point in time.

12 Hash Algorithm

In the blockchain world, you often hear about the term "hashing."

Let's examine what happens when "hashing" takes place. Take the 300,000-word *One Hundred Years of Solitude*, for example. "Hashing" means the compression of this 300,000-word novel into a few bytes through a hashing algorithm. The specific length depends on differing hashing algorithms.

The 300,000 words are the input, and the few bytes are the output. It is commonly understood that this "compression" process is called "hashing," and the output value is referred to as "a hash."

The most significant feature of "hashing" is irreversible. That means you can't deduce the input value through the output value. In other words, you can't get back the original text of *One Hundred Years of Solitude* in its uncompressed state through a few bytes.

Why? It is because, in the compression process, we have lost most of the details of *One Hundred Years of Solitude*. Therefore, it is impossible to deduce what kind of book the original text was or even determine whether it is a book.

For example, the mobile phone fingerprint recognition technology you use daily uses the hashing principle.

The pulp of your finger contains a lot of information about the uneven skin texture. It is impossible to record this information completely when the mobile phone collects your fingerprint for the first time.

Therefore, when the mobile phone collects fingerprints, it is actually "hashing once" to compress your massive fingerprint information into a relatively small data unit and record it. The fingerprint you finally enter into the mobile phone is equivalent to the compressed hash value.

By "hashing once," a small amount of information can represent your fingerprint, and the original and complete fingerprint information can't be reversed based on this amount of data.

However, this hashing isn't perfect. There are no two identical fingerprints in the real world. Even identical twins with the same DNA have different skin friction ridges and textures due to different acquired environments and development. Every friction ridge can be considered the

exclusive identity information of the finger's owner.

However, what is recorded of a finger is incomplete because the hashing algorithm has discarded most of the finger's friction ridges. Therefore, there is the possibility of two mobile phone users entering the same fingerprint ID, and this hash's coincidence is called a "hash collision" or "clash."

For example, Apple's public statement shows that the probability of fingerprint ID coincidence reaches 1/50,000. That is to say, one person in every 50,000 people can unlock your phone with his fingerprint. It sounds scary, right? But the reliability of mobile phone fingerprint identification technology can still be guaranteed at present because the probability of accidental association between people who share fingerprint IDs is extremely low.

Now, let's come back to the blockchain. It can be understood as an interlocking data chain. Each block header records the summary information of the previous block, which is actually its hash value. As long as the original data is slightly altered, the resulting hash value will be completely different, and conflicts will occur among the ledgers. That is the secret of the blockchain's security.

- **Related vocabulary**

  41. SHA-256
  75. Homomorphic Hashing

13 Mining

If the mineral mined in a gold mine is the said precious metal, cryptocurrency must be mined from a blockchain. "Mining" is a competition to "mine" new coins first. Those who participated in this competition were also vividly called "miners."

Of course, they don't have to work in dangerous mines like gold miners wearing miners' lamps. Instead, they finish their tasks using mining rigs.

Initially, the concept of mining applied to only Bitcoin. Bitcoins circulate in a blockchain network daily, but each new bitcoin can only be generated through mining.

If mining is regarded as a game between miners, Satoshi Nakamoto, as a game developer, set a very clever closed loop of rules from the very beginning. The generation of new bitcoins is also closely related to the transaction of old coins.

Now, let's assume you are a trader who initiated a bitcoin transfer and look at what happens next in the blockchain network and how the miners complete this mining competition.

First, the software you use to initiate the transaction broadcasts the transaction information to the blockchain network. But it doesn't mean that your transaction is immediately added to the blockchain, as it "floats" initially in the vast blockchain network.

Therefore, the transaction recipient will find that the bitcoins aren't received in real time, and they need to wait in severe anxiety for a while

before receiving the coins you transfer.

Why is this?

As mentioned before, blockchain is a data chain, and each block is a "box" filled with transaction data. A miner who chooses to transact with you must find a block to "encapsulate" the transaction before it can be connected to a blockchain.

However, the "box" that holds the data isn't readily available. Miners can see "old blocks" full of transactions on the blockchain, but now they are eager to get new blocks so that their selected transactions can be connected to the blockchain as soon as possible.

The process of mining is the mining of new blocks.

As a competition, the champion will, of course, be rewarded, and the prize for mining is the bitcoin. You often hear the expression "mining bitcoins," which, to be precise, means that miners receive bitcoin rewards after mining new blocks.

As you can imagine, this is undoubtedly tough competition because miners worldwide dream of getting their rewards. And the price of bitcoins today isn't the same as it was over a decade ago.

So, what kind of competition rules do they have to follow?

Satoshi Nakamoto is worthy of being a master of technology. He prepared an exceedingly complex math problem for miners.

Here is the math problem: The miners have already selected the transactions they want to place in a new block, and most of the information in its block header can be obtained by calculation.

Now, they need to find a number that hashes the other information in the block header to a value less than the value given by the software.

It is like a game of throwing dice with several people. There are two dice in total. Now, the rules of the game require that the sum of the two dice thrown is less than six. Whoever's dice thrown reaches a number less than six first will be the winner.

The process of finding this number is equivalent to blind guessing. Whoever guesses the qualified number the fastest can announce that he has succeeded in mining a new block.

14 Consensus Mechanisms

Blockchain is a super-giant ledger full of transaction information. This ledger isn't kept in the hands of an authoritative person. Nor can an individual administrator decide which data to add. Instead, it is controlled by millions of participants in the blockchain network and jointly supervised and kept by them.

This method avoids the rent-seeking corruption easy to breed in centralized systems. But it also presents some new challenges: Among the unfamiliar participants scattered all over the world, who will add the content of the ledger? How do you ensure the correctness of the additions in a trustless environment? And how to guarantee the consistency of the account book in everyone's hands?

At this point, you can only rely on a set of effective and reliable rules. Each participant makes decisions according to the rules.

This set of highly rational and self-disciplined rules is called a consensus mechanism. A common consensus mechanism comprises Proof of Work (PoW), Proof of State (PoS), and Delegated Proof of State (DPoS).

Let's briefly talk about PoW and PoS. Both these two consensus mechanisms include designed mining games. Whoever can first solve the system's mathematical puzzle has a higher probability of adding a new block to a blockchain. The only difference between the two consensus mechanisms lies in the essential factors determining who is more likely to solve the puzzle.

In the PoW mechanism used by Bitcoin, whether or not to solve the problem depends on the size of the computing power. In those public blockchains that use the PoS mechanism, the key factors that affect the outcome of the competition are the amount and duration of holding cryptocurrencies.

As for the trendy DPoS mechanism, it is a somewhat representative democracy, where participants vote to elect delegations with the right to add new blocks.

Different consensus mechanisms aim to maintain the blockchain network's safe operation through economic incentives. The reason is that only when maintaining the security of the blockchain network is more rewarding than attacking it will each participant be motivated to contribute to the network's security rather than making trouble in it.

Therefore, a set of rules that can achieve this ultimate goal can be regarded as an ideal consensus mechanism.

- **Related vocabulary**

32. PoW
33. PoS
34. DPoS

15 Ethereum

Some people refer to Ethereum as Bitcoin version 2.0, which is very misleading. The idea of developing Bitcoin indeed inspired Ethereum. But from the dual dimensions of function and ideal, there are huge differences between the two.

When Satoshi Nakamoto designed Bitcoin, he positioned it as a peer-to-peer payment system. His ideal is to establish a transaction model that can fully trust each other without a centralized institution's endorsement. So, Bitcoin is a currency symbol.

Later, people refined blockchain technology after studying Bitcoin design architecture. Then, a trend of technological thoughts inspired people to think more broadly. They asked if transaction records can be stored on different computers in a decentralized manner through blocks, then what else would be stored using this technology?

In 2013, Vitalik Buterin, a Russian-Canadian programmer who had just turned 19, cast another boulder after Bitcoin in this pond of a glamorous new field: Ethereum. The ripples he caused spread to the world beyond finance.

The technical solution he proposed is that the codes of various applications can be stored in the Ethereum network, such as transaction records. In other words, the development team can build blockchain applications based on the services provided by Ethereum. In layman's terms, the ideal of Ethereum can be seen as providing a set of "templates" for the development of blockchain applications.

It sounds similar to the open-source Android system, but the two are fundamentally different.

If you launch a mobile game application, most program code runs on the game company's server. All the code and data of an application developed on Ethereum, called a "Dapp," run on the Ethereum network. Since Ethereum is a decentralized network with blockchain as the underlying technology, even

Vitalik can't tamper with any code or data. All information is actually stored in the decentralized computers of participants in the Ethereum network.

On the other hand, the execution of DApps on Ethereum is no longer dominated by a central authority, and even the developer team of this program has no right to make rule changes unilaterally.

Now let's imagine such an application scenario together.

You must know the business logic of online car-hailing services: The service provider takes 20-30% of the finder's fee from the fare paid by passengers. But have you ever thought about why we need such a platform when taking a taxi and why we can't run to the street to wave a vacant car to stop? Perhaps, you may think that the platform charges the finder's fee only because it matches passengers with private automobiles having excess

capacity. You may also think we pay for the platform's scheduling and matching functions. But, in essence, it is also because the platform helps build trust between passengers and drivers.

We need such a platform to record the driver's identity and reduce the probability of him doing evil. As a passenger, you can't do whatever you want in the whole process, and the platform is also binding on you. The finder's fee we pay is actually the cost of trust.

Suppose there is now a development team that designs a blockchain ride-hailing DApp based on the "template" of the Ethereum network. In that case, ideally, the intermediary function will be eliminated, passengers and drivers will establish a peer-to-peer connection, and the passenger will use cryptocurrency to pay the driver directly. The result of the transaction is recorded on the Ethereum network. So will be the personal information of the passenger and driver, and all participants will jointly keep the transaction record. All the contracts of the taxi DApp are also permanently written into the Ethereum network.

In addition, it is free for programmers to develop apps on Android, but if they want to deploy their project on Ethereum and make it a DApp, they need to pay "Ether." Unlike deflationary bitcoins, the supply of ethers is unlimited because its primary value lies in its "use."

Of course, the blockchain taxi-hailing program just mentioned is only ideal. In fact, there are still loopholes in its logic: What if the driver provides false information to the Ethereum network at the beginning?

Blockchain can only guarantee that the information added to the chain can't be doctored. But this technology is by no means omnipotent because it can't ensure that the information provided is authentic and reliable.

Therefore, to put it into practice, the cooperation of the personal credit reporting system is needed, and the support of the social consensus is also essential. That is why the most significant proportion of Ethereum DApps are still games with the same "virtual" genes.

When things on and off the chain clash vehemently, there is still a long way to go before ideal DApps emerge.

Unlike Satoshi Nakamoto, who has vanished, the young father of Ethereum is often active in the public eye and has come to China many times. Besides, his father, who first preached Bitcoin to him, and his mother, whom the media call "an orator," treat cryptocurrencies' popularization as a family mission.

- **Related vocabulary**

  18. DApp

16 Smart Contracts

As early as 1993, computer scientist Nick Szabo proposed the concept of smart contracts. A smart contract is a pre-written computer code drawing up a contract stating explicitly the promises to be kept by the contracting parties. The code automatically executes the content of this contract.

For example, you rush sweating to the vending machine after a basketball match, put a coin in a vending machine, press a button corresponding to the product, and see a cold bottle of cola roll down from the shelf. It is a case of a vending machine executing a simple, smart contract.

For a long time, smart contracts haven't broken away from this simple form and are only limited to the primary "communication" between humans and machines. Some people imagined early on that a smart contract could be used in interpersonal networks and allow the transaction between people to conduct more complex value exchanges directly by bypassing the intermediate platform. However, the biggest problem is the high cost of building trust.

It is fair to say that the emergence of blockchain and the smart contract hit it off, resulting in the most fantastic chemical reaction. Smart contracts based on blockchain technology can't be secretly doctored because all the code is stored on the blockchain network. Not only is the execution of the contract automatically triggered, but anyone in the entire network can trace it back, which forms the basis of trust between strangers.

Therefore, we must say that it is the most advanced experiment in human attempts to reduce the cost of trust.

Smart contracts are used in currency, property, stocks, or any scenario where there is a transfer of value.

Smart contracts are used in currency, property, stocks, or any scenario where there is a transfer of value. For example, in crowdfunding, blockchain smart contracts can act like an unselfish, intelligent bad cop, hosting the funds that are successively transferred in, judging whether the amount has reached the set financing target, and then automatically executing the corresponding operations. You don't have to worry about a fund-embezzling "invisible hand" behind it.

If daily life in the future is more "blockchainized," you can also imagine a scenario: You are a *beipiao* renter. Incidentally, a *beipiao* lives and works in Beijing without a registered household status. You have signed a smart contract with your landlord and agreed to pay rent before a designated date. Otherwise, the password of the electronic lock on the door in your rented room will be changed without notice.

The whole process of the operation should be like this: You transfer a sum of cryptocurrency to the smart contract account, which triggers a function that sends a string of passwords used to open the door. You can enter the room by entering the passcode. It will automatically change once you are delinquent on your rent payment or have stopped renting the space.

Do you see? You no longer need an intermediary to intervene. The entire process is less cumbersome, and the transaction is so transparent and verifiable that the chance of a conflict between you and the landlord is lessened.

However, technology will continuously evolve by overcoming obstacles. Smart contracts also face enormous challenges. Since no one can tamper with and control the smart contract after execution, it isn't easy to remedy the loopholes in the code in time. The hordes of demons lurking in the dark can never be ignored.

17 Token

For a while, when you opened the news app, you often saw the buzzword "currency replacement" in news reports about blockchain. Like the "meal replacement" eaten by weight-losing fanatics, "currency replacement" sounds like a kind of replacement for cryptocurrency.

But then, people seemed to act in concert with the prior agreement and began to discuss *tongzheng*. It sounds more enigmatic than "currency replacement," only that it may cause people to associate it with *tongxingzheng,* which means something like a "pass." People wondered that tongzheng might refer to permission to allow entry and exit from a network.

In fact, either "currency replacement" or *tongzheng* means "token" in computer science. Token refers to a type of cryptocurrency in the context

of blockchain. DApps created on Ethereum, or other similar platforms, are issuing tokens.

Similar to the cryptocurrencies such as bitcoins and ethers, the core attributes of tokens are also decentralized. But the difference is that bitcoins and ethers have independent blockchain networks, whereas tokens can only work on platforms like Ethereum.

Let's take Ethereum as an example to see what role tokens can play.

Let's review the scenario of taxi-hailing services based on the blockchain I mentioned earlier. Now, the development team has deployed the program's code on the Ethereum network. While the smart contract is written, tokens are issued according to the "template" provided by Ethereum. The number of the tokens to be issued is written into the contract from the beginning. Please allow me to call these fictitious tokens "taxi coins." Passengers can pay "taxi coins" to taxi drivers. Usually, they can also use ethers instead.

If a passenger chooses the "taxi coin," the smart contract will record the usage. Miners will stuff every smart contract transaction into the blocks and connect them to the Ethereum network.

Do you see that in the taxi-hailing Dapp, "taxi coins" can be used "in place of" ethers, which may be why tokens are referred to as "currency replacement" in Chinese?

Tokens can be circulated and used in the ecosystem built by a program's application. In other words, a token has become a "pass" to operate in the ecosystem. That is why "Token" is also referred to as *tongzheng* (pass) in Chinese.

However, you can also find that a token is equivalent to a "sub-ecosystem" on Ethereum. Therefore, it will be highly challenging for tokens to gain broad recognition of their value and user base.

Many teams still choose to issue tokens to create a blockchain project due to the high cost of developing and maintaining an independent blockchain like Ethereum. Since tokens can also be issued with "a click of a button" on platforms like Ethereum, it is also swiftly used to transform some traditional business models.

Suppose blockchain technology is gliding toward the future of human society. In that case, the various possibilities at the application level constructed by tokens are beautiful and open valleys presented to ordinary people. Based on smart contracts, the threshold for expanding blockchain applications is lowered. If Satoshi Nakamoto portrays a romantic picture of decentralized freedom, the token gives this freedom a landing site.

- **Related vocabulary**

  98. Tokenization

18 DApp

The emergence of smartphones has made apps a roaring success, and the establishment of Ethereum has made the DApp a smash hit.

Simply put, DApps are applications running on the blockchain network. These programs include both projects that independently build a public blockchain like Bitcoin and projects that issue tokens. The letter "D" is short for "decentralization."

The front-end presentation of DApps is similar to that of regular apps, but the logic behind them is entirely different.

You may have understood from my previous introduction to Ethereum that the most significant difference between the two is that regular apps are controlled by the centralized computer of a specific company. In contrast, the code of DApps is stored in countless computers that are unfamiliar to each other.

So, the question is how this will benefit you as a user.

If you are a game player, you may have encountered such a problem: The

game company promises to release a particular top-level item in a limited amount. Tempted by the promise that you can change the battle situation, you have bought the item by tightening your belt but never seem to know if the promise can be honored.

Suppose it is a Dapp issued in a limited amount abiding by a smart contract. Once written in it, the rules can't be doctored. After being triggered, the smart contract will automatically issue the contracted amount of items. At the same time, the smart contract's release is also transparent and verifiable. A game company may reissue a smart contract with modified rules in the background, but the new contract's issuance can also be recorded on the chain, where it can be supervised.

You may have opened a familiar website and tragically see only the "404" status code. Downtime is possible when a code execution program is only stored on a centralized computer. In the case of a DApp, whose code is stored on computers across the network, others can execute the "launch" command for you. Downtime will cease if it is in a decentralized network with enough nodes.

However, because there is no central organization to interfere with the operation of the DApp, absent-minded people should pay particular attention: You usually only need a single password you set to log in to an app. But when you register on a DApp, it will also randomly issue you a string of numbers or letters, which is your only proof of identity on the blockchain network.

To optimize the user experience, DApps generally let you set your password, but once you switch to a new device, you must use the issued credentials to log in. Unfortunately, you can't touch your transaction information permanently stored in the DApp on the chain if you lose them.

In regular apps, you may be accustomed to clicking "forgot password" to get help because a centralized service keeps this information for you. In a blockchain, however, this kind of service no longer exists because you are the only keeper of your credentials.

In fact, one of the criteria for judging whether a DApp is valuable is whether the performance of "decentralization" is necessary for its application scenarios. While we have a penchant for a world that is always creative, there are also a lot of DApps that create just pseudo-needs.

Decentralization may be beautiful, but it probably only provides a new option for the world. It is because the decentralized-organization method will almost inevitably bring about a loss of efficiency. For example, the DApp user experience may not match that of ordinary apps. After all, the current apps have already turned us into impatient users. In a Dapp, you may have to wait for over ten minutes to get the desired service or product, even when you have paid cryptocurrency for them. The delay is because network participants must verify each operation's legitimacy jointly.

The world in the future is more likely to be one where centralization and decentralization coexist. The creation of each DApp must be carefully examined in terms of efficiency and fairness. Only when the latter becomes necessary in the DApp ecosystem will its value be genuinely supported.

19 Fiat Money

When we discuss "fiat money" in the context of blockchain, it means legal currency endorsed by government decrees.

Our common sense tells us that fiat money should have been related to gold and silver. Those precious metals are backed by their material value because even if they aren't used for exchange, they can still be smelted and cast into various other objects. Fiat money, however, has no corresponding material value.

Fiat money is merely a thin piece of paper, a small coin, or an intangible number string stored in a bank card or a mobile phone. Since the 18th century, various countries have issued their fiat money, which has today replaced almost all other forms of currency once in popularity.

The phenomenon also makes people gradually forget the essence of fiat money. Its value lies only in the public trust. Its value anchor would be lost due to the collapse of public trust. You may understand it this way: Once the government decree becomes invalid, the legal money' value will instantly vanish.

The scenario of people losing their trust in the Deutsche Mark occurred in post-Second World War Germany, whose economy collapsed. Since the government's credibility endorsed the fiat money, the country's defeat in the war and political self-examination led to Mark's severe depreciation, turning

it into a pile of waste paper. People would use cigarettes instead of banknotes as media of exchange in daily life.

Today, some countries severely lack government credibility and are plagued by persistent hyperinflation. So, they seek to use cryptocurrencies to rescue and reshape their monetary systems. Since cryptocurrency is based on mathematics and encryption laws, the rules from issuance to operation are stable. Therefore, those countries have found a sense of security in it.

20 Cryptocurrency and Digital Currency

In some media, the reference to the terms "cryptocurrency" and "digital currency" isn't rigorous. According to accurate translations, bitcoin, ether, and various "currencies" built with cryptography's support should belong to "cryptocurrency," that is, "encrypted currency."

Cryptocurrencies are often referred to as digital currencies in the media because they exist in a digital rather than physical form and, at the same time, have the property of being tradable. But strictly speaking, there is no globally unified definition of digital currency so far. Li Lihui, head of the Blockchain Research Working Group of China Internet Finance Association, believes that digital currency must belong to a country, enjoy sovereign endorsement, have a qualified issuer, and boast the support of a country's credibility.

Neither cryptocurrencies nor bitcoins can be called digital currencies according to this standard.

It is worth mentioning that the earliest cryptocurrency wasn't Bitcoin. In the 1990s, cryptography scholars invented a type of cryptocurrency linked to gold called "electronic gold."

In short, "electronic gold" means that users open an account on the Internet and remit some cash in exchange for the gold equivalent stored electronically. "Electronic gold" is operated behind the scenes by several companies, each of which issues its particular cryptocurrency, and the currency unit is generally named after the company.

However, unlike the Bitcoin network, which was later built on the underlying blockchain technology, no matter what kind of "electronic gold" it was, the previous cryptocurrencies were issued by centralized institutions.

Bitcoin was the first decentralized cryptocurrency. It isn't only borderless and uncontrolled, but its value is completely decoupled from physical objects. Have you found that it is very similar to fiat currency? Its value comes from the trust of its supporters.

Bitcoin is now the most widely accepted cryptocurrency in the world. While not officially recognized as a "currency" by the governments of most countries, some brick-and-mortar stores already accept bitcoins as a currency for payment.

Other cryptocurrencies that are also issued based on the support of decentralized technology are divided into two categories. One is a currency with an independent blockchain like Bitcoin and is issued as a currency realized through mining. The other is the token issued based on smart contracts on a blockchain like Ethereum. These tokens are only equivalent to the "passes" in the DApp ecosystem. They don't have currency attributes.

They are also called cryptocurrencies because they can be exchanged with physical objects.

- **Related vocabulary**

  97. CBDC

PART 2

Operation Mechanisms

21 Mining Rigs

Some mining rigs appear like cable converter boxes in metal consoles, while others are machines as large as refrigerators. However, their functions are the same.

Just like the various diamond panning and screening tools or oil-extracting devices, special equipment is required for "mining" some cryptocurrencies. You can understand mining rigs as the computers that "mine" the currencies.

Mining rigs may have gained some "following" now, but the earliest mining rigs were used to mine bitcoins. Therefore, you can better learn about mining rigs by understanding the "mining" of bitcoins.

Unlike physical petroleum, which requires drilling into the ground and extracting to the earth's surface, bitcoins are mined using mining rigs online.

Mining rigs are employed to solve complex mathematical problems. You can treat the process as "mining" the solutions to the problems. That is why it is called "mining."

The more powerful a mining rig is, the faster it can "mine" the correct solution to the problem. The first miner to "mine" the correct answer will be rewarded with bitcoins.

The rewarding process is also seen as part of the process of bitcoin mining.

In the real world, petroleum-extracting machinery has been upgraded

several generations to extract oil more efficiently. For example, the equipment has become so advanced that oil can be drawn out from over ten thousand meters beneath the earth's surface. Bitcoin mining rigs are also being upgraded constantly.

In the early days, the competition for computing power wasn't fierce due to the small number of people participating in bitcoin mining. Even Satoshi Nakamoto himself could mine bitcoins through the CPU of a home computer. With the continuous expansion of Bitcoin's influence, the number of participants has increased significantly, intensifying the competition and demanding more computing power. Mining rigs with customized performance have emerged as required.

22 ASIC

ASIC is short for Application Specific Integrated Circuits. "Specific" means that the application is designed for a specific purpose. In our discussion of blockchain and cryptocurrencies, we refer to ASIC as a chip specially designed for mining rigs.

Mining rigs are tools to "mine" cryptocurrencies. We can imagine bitcoins as the rich minerals buried deep beneath the earth's surface. A mining rig continuously calculates complex mathematical problems to find the correct solutions. "Getting" the correct answer is figuratively called "mining."

The specifications of the chips in the mining rigs directly affect mining efficiency. Especially in a game where many players compete, each has the incentive to keep upgrading his rigs.

Of course, Satoshi Nakamoto and his early followers never used mining rigs with ASIC chips. Because of the lack of competitors, they just relied on their home desktops to win bitcoin rewards.

You must know that the CPU (Central Processing Unit) is equivalent to the "brain" of a computer and can handle a variety of tasks. But soon, people discovered that mining, a way of calculating math problems, was merely doing repetitive labor, which has a single purpose and is purely mechanical. CPU isn't the best choice for the job. It is like an athlete who can be a "Triathlon" champion is judged by his long-distance running only, so the judgment may not be the best.

Therefore, GPU (Graphic Processing Unit), once dedicated to processing images, caught people's attention and entered the "race of mining rigs."

Compared with the CPU, the GPU's function is unitary, and its processing logic is unsophisticated. When it is used to process massive mathematical calculations for rendering graphics, it is much more efficient than the CPU bogged by multiple tasks.

As a result, mining rigs entered the GPU era.

GPU hasn't been buried in the history of mining rigs until today. However, a contemporary rig with brand-new logic became the GPU's

competitor. Such a rig could be customized by users able to write their programmable logic, known as FPGA (Field Programmable Gate Array). It turned a mining rig into a Lego set, the construction of which is up to a child's imagination.

However, although there were some conceptual breakthroughs in the technology, FPGA had its drawbacks: insufficient computing power and difficulty in its development. As a result, it didn't enjoy a long life and eventually found its way to the mining rig museum.

A better and more comprehensive alternative is ASIC.

Like FPGA, ASIC can also be specially customized for the algorithm required for mining. But the computing power, power consumption, and development threshold have been qualitatively optimized, so it has been a brilliant achievement in the history of mining rigs.

Now, let's forget the "transitioning" FPGA and compare the CPU, the GPU, and the ASIC with some examples.

Suppose you are a gourmet and have an idea of a few restaurant choices: first, a buffet in a five-star hotel that serves dishes of Chinese, Western, and Japanese cuisines; second, a home-style eatery featuring the evocation of nostalgia for customers' childhood; and third, a social-media influencer's closed-door restaurant featuring excellent delicacies. In that case, which will you pick?

Like the five-star hotel buffet, the CPU is more adaptive and suitable for customers who prefer tasting various dishes. The GPU is comparable to a particular cuisine, offering dishes less diverse than the buffet, but each is better prepared. ASIC is the dishes fixed by the closed-door restaurant catering to each customer's taste.

Comparing their computing powers, one can see the superiority of ASIC, customized for mining. The computing power of a CPU is about 10MH/s (10×10^6 hashes per second), whereas the computing power of a GPU is about 500MH/s (500×10^6 hashes per second). As of the end of 2019, the computing power of the ASIC dedicated to calculating bitcoins can reach 70TH/s (70×10^{12} hashes per second).

23 Accounting

Suppose an "Outstanding Contribution Award" is granted in a blockchain network. In that case, miners worldwide should be the recipients because they are responsible for the dirty job of maintaining the regular operation of the entire blockchain network, not limited to mining.

As in real life, many daily transactions come to pass in the blockchain network. Since transactions exist, there is a need for a widely accepted bookkeeper.

Miners are responsible for bookkeeping in a blockchain.

In real life, when you conduct a direct cash transaction with someone, the transaction is recorded on your and the other person's account books, be they paper ledgers or memories. The deal can't be denied in the future if you have written a receipt to the other party.

When you use a bank card to transact with a person, you pick the bank to keep the record. The bank database tracks and maintains the transaction ledger.

If someone denies the transaction in the future, you only need to ask for the day-to-day statement of the two bank accounts and check where the money is.

You may understand the process as the role of the bank as a bookkeeper who endorses your transaction's authenticity with its credibility.

Blockchain is a data chain regarded as a giant ledger. But its uniqueness lies in the absence of a "central institution" like the bank to record your transaction. That is because the blockchain network is decentralized.

Mining explains how new blocks linked to a blockchain are born. Then, the miners' action of entering their transaction data into new blocks and linking them to the blockchain by the miners is called bookkeeping.

Then, why are miners reliable bookkeepers since they aren't the "central institutions"?

Because when a miner mines a new block and enters his transaction data, other miners will verify if the block conforms to the rules of the mining game and if the transaction is legitimate. They do so to avoid adding their blocks to an illegal block.

It is like a cash transaction. You will check to ensure that the bank notes the other party has paid you aren't counterfeits. Simultaneously, the bank will also check if there are sufficient funds in the transfer account and if the account's address and name are genuine.

The miner won't be awarded bitcoins if a problem is found. Other miners will also reject his block to prevent it from being added to the blockchain.

On the other hand, when you initiate a bitcoin transfer, you need to pay a miner fee, which is equivalent to the transfer fee charged by traditional banks. This money will be given to the miners helping you add your transaction data to the block and link it to the blockchain.

If other miners can't verify his mined block, his miner's fee will be lost. Therefore, no rational miner will maliciously add illegal transaction records to the blocks under this economic incentive mechanism.

Thanks to this mechanism, blockchain finds a trusted bookkeeper for every transaction.

24 Miner

When introducing the concepts of mining and accounting, we mentioned the miner, the executor of the two operations.

You can say they are the miners of every block and the operators who actually seal your transaction information into the blockchain network.

They are well-deserved "model workers" because they are also the custodians of the complete ledger of the blockchain network. They are responsible for checking the legitimacy of each transaction, with a workload no less than the counterfeit money detector behind the glass screen of a bank counter.

However, no so-called "employers" pay salaries to these miners working around the clock, contributing significantly to the blockchain network. Yet, that doesn't dampen the enthusiasm of these contributors in the slightest.

Instead, they pride themselves on working for a fully decentralized economic incentive mechanism.

Miners get their rewards directly from the blockchain network without asking for them. Neither do they know who pays them as a token of thanks.

The first financial return for a miner is a batch of bitcoins rewarded to him for mining each new block. As the pioneer of the entire Bitcoin kingdom, Satoshi Nakamoto has already set clear reward rules: For each batch of

210,000 blocks generated, the reward for mining will decrease by half. Since a block is mined every ten minutes on average, the reward is approximately halved every four years.

He received 50 bitcoins for the first block he mined, and the latest reward amount was attenuated per the above rules.

The number of bitcoins is constant, and no new bitcoins will be issued. So, this rule also means that the mining reward will eventually become naught. But it doesn't mean that the incentive for miners will disappear.

That is because every time they help with bookkeeping, they also get a reward called the "miner fee." It still exists even when the bitcoin reward disappears. It is the second financial reward miners can get.

The actual payer of the miner fee is a cryptocurrency transaction's initiator, who determines the specific amount.

Miners always prefer to record transactions with higher miner fees. Higher fees will result in speedy transaction processing and also accelerated confirmation.

The blockchain network's beauty lies in the operation of the network based on the autonomous economic incentive model.

Illegal information a miner inserts into a block is destined to fail the inspection by other miners due to the conflict of the ledger. When this happens, he can't get the miner fee, losing his invested computing power.

Since a miner's conduct is bound by his economic interests, the probability of him doing evil decreases accordingly.

25 Mining Farms

When I explained miners, you knew that bitcoin mining was an increasingly competitive race of mining rigs.

In fact, the key to winning the competition depends not only on the performance of mining rigs' hardware but also on the number of rigs.

That is because mining is essentially a game of probability. Under the premise of the same model of rigs, the more they are, the greater the possibility of mining bitcoins.

In the earliest period of bitcoin mining, individual geeks worked alone at their two-square-meter desks. If they could afford a palm-size mining rig, they could mine bitcoins. But a single or a few mining rig's computing power was extremely limited.

Some "nouveau riches" and companies purchased a large number of mining rigs, placing hundreds of them together in a centralized site, and this physical space is called a "mining farm."

All these mining farms are located "remotely." For example, some are on the lava plains near the Arctic Circle, and others have found their way to the unknown wilderness in the Columbia Basin.

In China, mining farms are likely set up in a gray and dilapidated factory next to a small hydropower station in the Southwest. When the dry season arrives, the farm owners will probably relocate their farms like migratory birds to places like Inner Mongolia or Xinjiang.

They may do this because they need to find cheap electricity sources. The highest cost of a mining farm isn't the mining rigs or workforce but the electricity the mining rigs consume when processing a large amount of computation.

26 Hash Rate

Hash rate is the ability to calculate the hash value originating from bitcoin mining. It is proportional to successfully mining a new block in unit time. In the same amount of time, the greater the hash rate, the more likely it

is that new blocks will be mined.

What is the reason for the phenomenon?

From the interpretation of mining, you have already learned that "mining a new block" is essentially a mathematical calculation process. Miners need to calculate the hash value in the header of a new block to meet the conditions set by the rules.

After a miner selects the transaction to be entered in a new block, most of the data in the block header can be determined, but the miner must fill in one particular datum by himself. Without shortcuts, he can only try to guess the number repeatedly until he can get the block header's hash value smaller than what is provided by the rule, winning the championship and getting the reward of bitcoins and miner fees.

Because the whole process is random, the greater the hash rate, the faster the hash value is calculated and the better chance a miner will have to calculate the required value first.

Hash rate is the ability to calculate how many hashes per second.

It is as if you left an important item in the classroom, and the school caretaker gave you a bunch of keys hanging in the gatehouse. It was up to you to figure out which key was the one that could unlock your classroom.

In this case, you had to try out each key. Since the process was random, the faster you worked with your hands, the more likely you would retrieve your item earlier.

The hash rate is equivalent to how fast you work with your hands.

- **Related vocabulary**

  12. Hash Algorithm

27 Mining Pool

Every miner is competing for computing power. Miners who can successfully mine blocks win bitcoin rewards, while other competitors at the same time get nothing. The efforts they spent on the computation to solve the mystery were all in vain. They could only pay the high electricity bill with tears and set about mining the next block.

With the existence of mining farms, fewer and fewer miners could win the hash rate crown with one or several mining rigs. The mining pool thus came into being.

Unlike the mining farm, the mining pool doesn't exist in physical space. But you can imagine it as a virtual "pool" with water coming from a river, a lake, or a sea. The mining pool is designed to pull the scattered miners' hash rate together to mine "in a group."

The scenario is similar to the challenging monsters in a role game. Players fight them with concerted efforts in teams. The game software will group the multiple characters logged into the platform into a team to counter the monsters and allow the team members to "carve up" the experience and equipment according to their contribution after winning the game.

However, the miners in the mining pool don't have a division of labor like the game players. They only accumulate their workload.

Mining pools also have unique revenue distribution mechanisms, varying with different mining pools.

Some mining pools distribute revenue based on the computing power contributed by each miner after successful mining. Due to the uncertainty of the mining results, miners' benefits match their risks.

Some mining pools also pay a fixed salary to the miners who provide computing power. On the one hand, the miners can "be guaranteed to receive their income no matter what happens," On the other hand, they will also be charged a higher handling fee to pay for the risks that the mining pools take on their behalf.

Some other mining pools additionally reward miners with more loyalty. Miners working in a particular mining pool for a long time can get extra benefits by contributing the same computing power.

28 Cloud Mining

Though mining farms and pools can pull together massive hash rates, there is still a risk of fruitlessness in mining. Computing power tycoons then have figured out a way to share the risk.

They "sell" some of the computing power online. Some people interested in mining revenue but unwilling to buy and maintain mining rigs can

participate in the mining game by purchasing hashing powers.

Despite the word "mining" in the name "cloud mining," it is actually more of a financial product.

Strictly speaking, purchasers of hashing powers can't be regarded as miners. Without mining rigs, they have only bought the mining services from mining farms or pools, and the miners from these companies do the dirty job of mining on their behalf.

It is like you want to invest in stocks but don't have time to study the stock market yourself, so you buy a fund product linked to the stock market, and the fund manager handles it for you. The more shares you buy, the greater your profit or loss.

Buying hashing power online is the mainstream cloud mining method, but buying such a service is risky.

Since mining farms or pools state that they sell you hashing powers without proof, "stealing of the powers" may occur. You can only estimate your due income based on the hashing power of the entire network.

For example, if the entire network's hashing power is 1000, and yours is 1, you should get an average of one-thousandth of the income. Your computing power may have been stolen if the deviation is too large.

However, due to lack of supervision, it is difficult to recover the loss even if you discover the malpractice. What you can do may only expose it online to help others avoid making the same mistake.

29 DDA

It must have been his whimsical decision: Satoshi Nakamoto kept the interval between the birth of every two new blocks at about ten minutes. It means that the time spent on mining new blocks is roughly limited to a designated period, however hard the multiple miners work simultaneously.

It is like these monks eating their soups: Whether ten monks eating 100 bowls or a hundred monks eating ten bowls, the time they spend eating the soup must be the same. Suppose they can all eat the same amount of soup. In that case, more people will usually spend less time finishing it. The difficulty level of soup eating must be adjusted to keep the duration of time consistent. For example, the monks are required to chant sutras while eating.

The same goes for bitcoin mining. When more people participate in mining, that is, when the hashing power of the entire network increases, the mining difficulty will also increase accordingly to maintain the interval between mining every two new blocks at about 10 minutes. If there are fewer miners, the mining will ease up consequently.

What exactly does this difficulty mean? As explained earlier, mining is finding a number that makes the block header's hash value less than the target value given by the rule. The DDA (Dynamic Difficulty Adjustment) of mining is to adjust the size of this target value.

It is like a game of throwing dice with several people. Now the rules of the game require that the sum of the two dice thrown is less than six, and whoever throws it first wins. In this game, "six" is the target value. The size of this target value determines the difficulty of the game: The larger the target value, the lower the difficulty, and vice versa. You can think about it. Isn't it less challenging to get the sum of the two dice smaller than ten?

The adjustment strictly follows a set of established rules.

The target value is adjusted every 2,016 blocks. Since all the 2,016 blocks are generated at intervals of 10 minutes, each adjustment takes 20,160 minutes, less than two weeks.

The difficulty adjustment criterion is the comparison of the time it takes to generate the latest 2,016 blocks with the expected time.

If participating miners are numerous, and their time is less than two weeks, the system will automatically make things more difficult by reducing the target value. Otherwise, it will increase the target value.

It is actually like the situation in some games. To provide a better playing experience, game developers also make corresponding adaptations to its difficulty to make players feel that the game is neither too difficult nor easy. The specific method is making real-time adjustments to the challenge according to the player's level.

If a player becomes skillful after gaining a lot of experience, the game's difficulty will increase, making the player feel that the game is always new.

If a player happens to be not up to the task, the game will automatically reduce the difficulty so that he won't lose enthusiasm for the game due to disappointment.

30 Orphan Blocks

If you have an in-depth understanding of the work of bitcoin miners, you will highly appreciate the whole set of reward mechanisms established by Satoshi Nakamoto. That is because miners not only have to work monotonously with repeated calculations on the mining rigs, but they also have to take the risk of getting no reward at all. Sometimes, "inherent problems or mistakes" would cause them to lose the bitcoin "prizes" by a slim chance.

Now, you have to put up with my request that you play this unlucky miner for a while.

You have successfully mined your first block, and the bitcoin reward contained in the block is beckoning to you. All you need to do is broadcast the mined block information to the blockchain network. You can't wait to inform other miners working hard to mine this same block, telling them you are a step ahead and that they can stop what they are doing to mine the next block in time.

Just at the juncture when victory is in sight, you tragically discover that another miner who mined the same block almost simultaneously has notified the blockchain network earlier than you due to network delay. What will happen next will devastate you.

There is such a rule in Bitcoin or other cryptocurrency blockchain networks: When multiple miners are mining two or more new blocks simultaneously, only one block will be recognized and retained. And it must always be the block connecting the most blocks behind it.

Since the miner with a smoother network publicized his success a little faster than you, the news that he mined a new block ahead of you was more quickly confirmed by other miners. They then connected the blocks they had mined to your lucky competitor's mined block one by one, keeping lengthening the chain.

You find that you were the first to mine a new block, even on the objective axis of time, but everyone abandoned it because it didn't form the longest chain. What are you feeling right now? Are you feeling lonely? Everyone will considerately call the block you have mined an "orphan block."

Orphan blocks are meaningless in the Bitcoin world. They are equivalent to the space junk produced by dysfunctional artificial satellites floating into oblivion in the vast void.

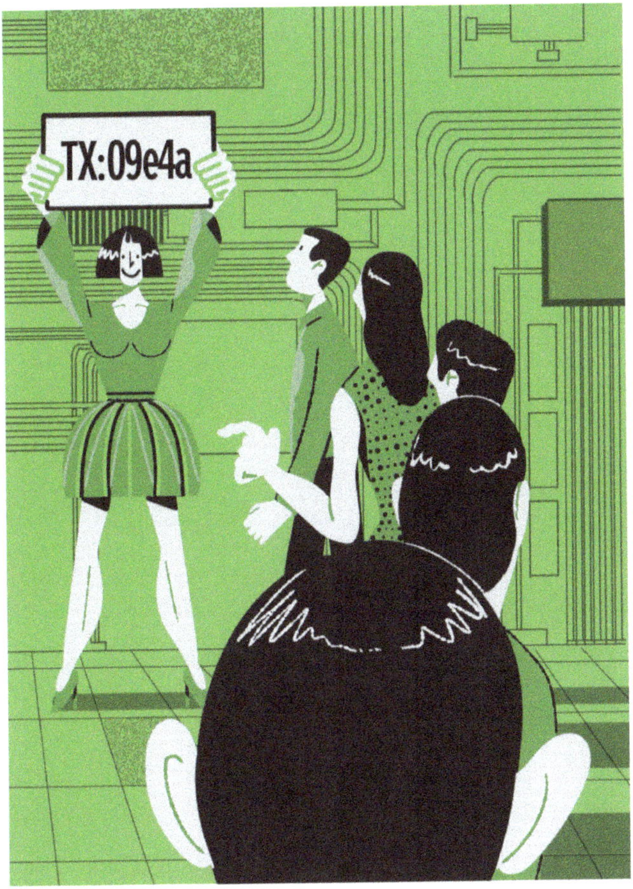

Orphaned blocks on the Ethereum blockchain aren't all that miserable, though. If other miners have filled in the information related to this orphan block in their newly mined blocks, they have proved the existence of this orphan block, and the "owner" of the orphan block may still receive a small amount of mining reward.

Behind the "humanized" design of Ethereum, there is a set of logic for security considerations. The interval for generating new blocks on Ethereum is much shorter than that of Bitcoin: It takes only ten seconds compared to the Bitcoin blockchain network, where the interval is about ten minutes. Such a short time dramatically increases the probability of producing orphan blocks. Scrapping them all would throw new-block-mining miners into chaos.

Since the public blockchain is a decentralized network, the high degree of autonomy allows each chain to have the opportunity to set and improve its criteria and build its network as a unique and brilliant presence.

31 Empty Blocks

Miners always try to squeeze as much transaction data as possible into a block because the more they do so, the more total miner fees they can earn. In a free and pure ecosystem supported by code, "interest" is the most reliable logic.

However, some blocks on the Bitcoin blockchain only contain the transaction that records the miner's withdrawal of the bitcoin reward without

any accounting information. Such blocks are called empty blocks.

Why are there seemingly wasteful empty blocks?

You may need to explore the details of the bitcoin mining mechanisms a little deeper. Suppose you are currently a miner buried in "solving the problems." The mining rigs work ferociously doing the calculations, hoping to quickly find the number closest to the target value set by the rules of the game.

"Ding-dong!" You suddenly received a message that the "next-door neighbor" had just mined a new block. Well, you must give up the computing at hand and get ready to mine the next block.

However, before doing this, you also need to download the block mined by the next-door miner to see what transaction data is already in it because you can't insert the same transaction information in the next block.

When mining, you and the next-door miner prioritized the transactions that paid the most accounting fees in the network. So, you have to wait patiently for a while to avoid overlapping. You know very well that if you repackage a transaction already packaged, even if you mine the next block, other miners on the network can't verify this block. This situation is more embarrassing than two movie stars dressed similarly meeting each other on the same red carpet.

Of course, you can't just watch your previous efforts go to waste, so you can only "check" the block mined by the next-door miner to ensure that you won't reenter the same transaction information.

Tx:12e4fe
Tx:10d45e
Tx:60d4e
Inp

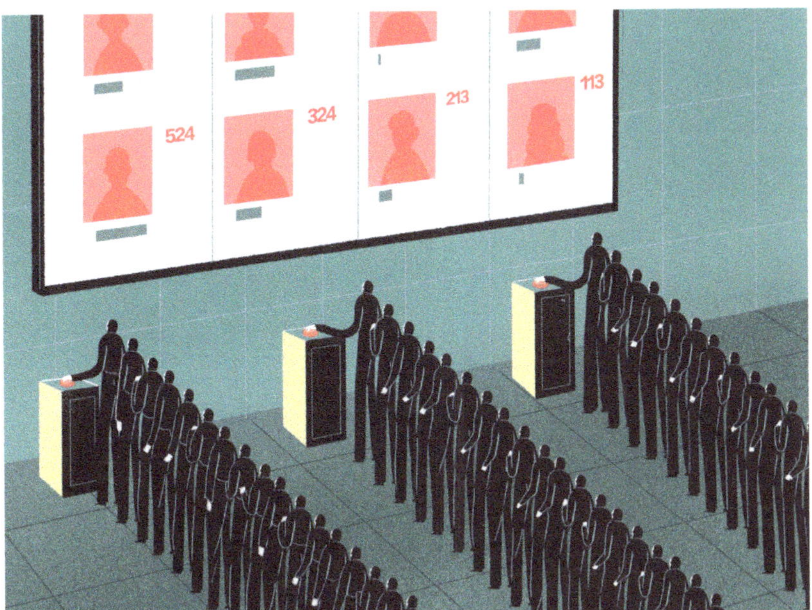
524
324
213
113

Although this act of downloading and "checking" takes only a few seconds, mining is a game where every second counts. As long as the mining rig is on, a miner must mine as much as possible. Let's assume you strike luck in these few seconds and happen to mine a new block.

Then, you may consider that you would rather leave the mined block empty than "wear the same attire" (enter the same transaction information) to have no gains. After all, Satoshi Nakamoto didn't stipulate that empty blocks can't be added to the blockchain network. You can still get bitcoin rewards. Unfortunately, you have to give up the miner fees, though.

After understanding empty blocks, you can see that too many can congest the network because a transaction waiting to be packaged and entered in a block will miss an opportunity to be packaged. Therefore, the bitcoin mining software is upgraded to shorten the waiting time for downloading and "checking" and compress the original few seconds as much as possible. This practice will reduce the probability of the mining rigs accidentally mining a new block during these seconds. That is how the blockchain network controls the rate of producing empty blocks.

32 PoW

PoW is short for Proof of Work. It is similar to an academic certificate that can prove how much effort you have put into your studies. PoW demonstrates how much effort a miner has put into mining.

The ultimate consensus reached by each consensus mechanism is actually a set of rules about who has the right to add new blocks to a blockchain.

PoW is the oldest of the rules because the Bitcoin network uses it. So far, many loyal followers of PoW still believe it is the purest and fairest decentralized consensus mechanism.

This consensus mechanism states that when all miners work hard to mine a new block, the winner provides the most PoW.

Every follower of the PoW consensus mechanism agrees that the miner who has done the most work has the highest probability of mining a new block.

A miner's work is quite dull, and there are no shortcuts. They keep hashing, trying to find a number that meets Nakamoto's rules as soon as possible. Because of this mining feature, the PoW consensus mechanism finally rewards the most "hard-working" miners.

How hard do miners have to work to mine blocks? We can look at some early blocks with the most lenient requirements, which required a mining rig to perform 232 calculations on average to mine a block.

By 2018, the average number of operations had neared 16 trillion times more, and that scary number keeps climbing.

The institutional model of bitcoin miners' "labor" is similar to diamond miners' bloody and teary toil. Cruel supervisors count the diamonds the workers panned and check if they have finished a certain amount of work at the end of the day.

A worker may be lucky enough to extract a sizable diamond, but the probability is slim. On the following day, the previous day's workload won't be accumulated, and the workload of a new workday needs to be recalculated.

Only one miner can mine a block while others competing simultaneously for a new block have to see their work come to nothing. Therefore, this pure hashing power PK (Player Kill) mechanism may guarantee the network's property of decentralization to the greatest extent. But it also causes a waste of power resources, which has become an object of public denunciation.

33 PoS

Among the many consensus mechanisms of blockchain, PoW is the earliest one. In the third year after Bitcoin emerged, another consensus mechanism was born. It was PoS, an abbreviation of "Proof of Stake." Stake means rights.

If a cryptocurrency adopts the PoS mechanism, it means that only those who hold the cryptocurrency can vote for the right to add new blocks. This competition isn't open to everyone in the blockchain network.

That is because proponents of this mechanism believe that only those who genuinely have a stake will be more willing to keep the blockchain network secure than to attack it. In contrast, in the PoW mechanism, miners competing for the right to add new blocks don't necessarily hold the cryptocurrency.

It is like a company's shareholding system, where those with more shares have greater rights and interests. The PoS mechanism also follows the principle of "the greater the shares, the greater the rights and interests."

This mechanism also exists in cryptocurrency mining games. The determinator of the games' winning rate is no longer "hard work," as required by the PoW mechanism, but the amount of cryptocurrency. The more currency one holds, the greater the chance of one's obtaining the right to add new blocks.

You can imagine a lottery player buying a lottery ticket. If everyone has a lottery ticket, everyone has the same probability of winning. But some lottery players purchase multiple lottery tickets at once to increase their chances of winning. A lottery player with 100 lottery tickets is more likely to succeed than a lottery player with ten.

The PoS mechanism may not require miners to work hard mining and thus save a lot of electricity. But it comes at the expense of the "pureness" of the PoW mechanism. People who hold more coins are more likely to mine new blocks and get mining rewards, thus becoming "wealthier." This Matthew effect will weaken the decentralization of blockchains that employ this consensus mechanism.

However, this mechanism is also evolving through continuous experimentation. Some cryptocurrency services that pursue the PoS mechanism have taken some countermeasures. For example, some also consider the length of holding the currency. This variable, called "coin age," is the product of the possessed coins' amount and duration. Blocks newly mined will offset part of the possessing time and cause the coin age to be recalculated.

Some cryptocurrency services also stipulate that after obtaining the right to add a new block, it is necessary to wait for a period before participation in the mining competition again is allowed.

These rules are all designed to eliminate monopoly as much as possible within the consensus framework of PoS.

34 DPoS

DPoS is short for Delegated Proof of Stake. It is a consensus mechanism that references the concept of election.

Under this mechanism, each token possessor doesn't directly participate in adding new blocks but votes for candidates. The candidates who have won the most votes can act as delegates and, in turn, add new blocks, serving as the miners in the PoW and PoS consensus mechanisms.

Let's look at what the delegates in the DPoS mechanism are doing.

Greater responsibility comes with greater power. Delegates with the right to add new blocks must maintain the security of the entire blockchain network, so they have to pay high fees yearly. After all, no one will vote for a candidate with aging mining rigs and worrying internet speeds.

In other words, only those who can afford the cost are eligible to apply as candidates. It is reminiscent of the U.S. presidential election. In reality, there are nearly 40 political parties in the United States, but why do the Democrats and the Republicans always take turns governing?

One of the fundamental reasons is that the cost of running for the presidency is enormous, and small parties aren't only unable to bear the burden themselves and have difficulty gaining the behind-the-scenes support of big chaebols.

Back to the DPoS consensus mechanism, each token holder can vote for no more than a certain number of candidates in the voting phase. Similar to PoS, the voting weight of each token holder isn't the same. The more tokens held, the greater the right to speak.

Therefore, DPoS is essentially an improvement of the PoS mechanism. As far as decentralization is concerned, its purity may be diluted to a certain extent, but it strikes a balance between purity and the requirements for efficiency.

When the delegates are selected, new blocks' addition doesn't require competition. So, new blocks are added significantly faster, and transactions are processed more quickly.

On the other hand, when the delegates complete a round of adding new blocks, the order of the next round will be randomly divided again to avoid delegates' fraudulent behavior as much as possible. Thus, the cost of the delegates conspiring to do evil will significantly increase.

If a delegate fails to perform his duties, such as not adding blocks within the designated time, there is a good chance he will lose during the subsequent voting stage.

The emergence of DPoS can be regarded as the participants' continuous self-renewal efforts in a decentralized public blockchain network.

The three variables of high efficiency, decentralization, and scalability have always been considered the "impossible triangle" that can't be realized simultaneously. Participants are always trying to find a set of game rules that can convince the public and run smoothly. And just like in the real world, wisdom lies in how to find the optimal solution.

Since the entire public blockchain network is highly autonomous, a persuasive consensus mechanism has the most fundamental charm. I believe that its exploration will never stop.

35 Byzantine Generals Problem

In the extensive blockchain transaction network, there is no authority to decide how to add new blocks that package transaction information. All decisions are made by consensus among participants. However, there may be evildoers among the participants to destroy the consensus. As early as 1982, some scholars compared this dilemma to a vivid story model called the "Byzantine Generals Problem."

The story model goes like this: The Byzantine Empire had many armies, each far apart. Their generals couldn't sit around at a fireside to discuss military strategies. So, they could only pass messages through messengers.

When it was necessary to attack other countries, they may be outnumbered and suffer a disastrous defeat if the generals acted discordantly. So, each general wrote his decision on whether to attack or retreat in a letter and sent it to other generals. The practice is equivalent to a vote. After receiving all the letters, the generals could advance or retreat in unison by following the majority's decision. It seemed simple if the generals were true to what they communicated and the enemy didn't intercept the messenger on his way.

But in the real world, they might be traitors among the generals or the messengers to confuse the consortium of command.

Let's assume there were five generals, and one of them was a traitor. Two generals voted to attack, while another two voted to retreat. The traitor, however, expressed his support for the decisions of both groups of generals respectively.

The two generals who chose to attack would do so because they had three votes for the offense. The other two generals would make the opposite decision because they had three votes for retreat.

The poor Byzantine generals had a conundrum: How would loyal generals agree on a strategy when they had traitors among them?

By analogy to the blockchain network, each participant in the consensus is equivalent to a general in the Byzantine generals problem, and the communication channel between them is tantamount to a messenger.

The need for blockchain participants to solve the problem of a consensus being destroyed by malicious nodes is the need to solve the Byzantine Generals Problem.

36 PBFT

PBFT is short for Practical Byzantine Fault Tolerance. It is a consensus mechanism commonly used in the consortium blockchain.

There may be perpetrators among those who participate in forming the consortium blockchain. "Fault tolerance" means that this mechanism is used to "tolerate" the existence of a certain number of malicious nodes so that they won't affect the expected achievement of the entire consensus.

As explained in Byzantine Generals Problem, a group of generals who can't meet wants to send the voting results through messengers to ensure concerted efforts to attack or retreat. But the mechanism can't prevent treasonous "bad generals" among them from attempting sabotage.

If the operating principle of PBFT is applied, the total number of generals would be increased to three times the "bad generals." Then, there

would be no interference in the generation of consensuses.

For example, if seven of the ten generals are "good," the voting result would be credible.

All of this is guaranteed by the PBFT algorithm, which, in a nutshell, requires that consensus participants pass votes to each other.

In a consortium blockchain using PBFT, the perpetrators are equivalent to "bad generals." As long as the total number of consensus participants on the blockchain is three times the number of the bad generals, regular operation of the system can be maintained.

37 Coinbase Transaction

The literal meaning of Coinbase seems to be "the foundation of the coin." Each Bitcoin block records the data of a transaction, and the first deal is called a Coinbase transaction.

However, an ordinary cryptocurrency transfer transaction you initiate can never become a Coinbase transaction because yours is prepared only for miners. It only records the information that the miner who first mines a block gets his reward.

Well, let's return to our digital world. As in a game of building a sequence of Chinese proverbs, where the first character is always produced by whim, Coinbase transactions are also automatically "issued" through the Bitcoin protocol. Since the miner-rewarding bitcoins are newly mined, there is no history of the transaction circulating layer by layer. Therefore, unlike other transaction data in the block, which also contains the "source" information, it only includes the "going to" information: the payment address filled in by miners themselves.

Some funny geeks write their innermost feelings in the blank for "source." The most famous words from the heart are left by Satoshi Nakamoto, the Father of Bitcoin. He used this tiny space to ridicule the financial crisis caused by centralized institutions. It is timeless because it is tamper-proof.

Interestingly, Bitcoin and the continuously refined and evolving blockchain games he invented have filled an enormous gap in human

currency and technology history.

38 Transaction

In the blockchain world, we often hear the word "transaction." However, unlike the daily actions of money and goods exchange, blockchain transactions refer to sending a virtual request. For example, when you transfer a bitcoin to your friend, you initiate a transaction, which includes your transfer address, your friend's address, the amount, and digital signatures. "Transaction" is a combination of these virtual pieces of information.

Whenever a cryptocurrency transaction information is inserted into a block and connected to a blockchain, someone's account "balance" will change, and the accounts of everyone in the current blockchain network will be updated to a new status. Therefore, in a broad sense, a transaction is a set of information pieces that change the current state of the blockchain network.

However, transactions aren't just used to describe changes in cryptocurrency balances. You must understand that when blockchain applications extend beyond cryptocurrencies, the ledger and transactions we are talking about are no longer linked to cryptocurrencies only.

Ethereum, for example, is used to store computer programs called DApps, not for payment only. DApp developers can deploy applications on the Ethereum network. The process of users using the applications is equivalent to changing the Ethereum ledger's status. It is executed by users sending transactions behind the scenes.

Take a chess-playing DApp, for example. To make a move, you need to send a transaction. This piece of information contains the smart contract you want to execute and which commands in the contract you want to execute. It also includes the parameters needed to be passed, such as where to place the chess piece, to use the extended metaphor.

The "when you moved what piece" content will appear on Ethereum after you send this transaction to the blockchain. The entire blockchain status is updated repeatedly in this way. Therefore, "transaction" isn't in the narrow sense of transferring ethers between users in Ethereum. It also includes various requests users send to smart contracts and pass between multiple smart contracts.

PART 3

Blockchain Microcosmos

39 Timestamps

A timestamp is mainly used to mark time, and "stamp" means "an official mark indicating genuineness and validity."

Timestamps in the digital world can be compared to postmarks in the real world. When people go to a post office to send a letter, the office will stamp the postage stamp. The content of the rubber stamp includes a specific place, the postal office's name, and a particular date. It shows that the postal office received the letter on that date.

In some kidnapping movies, you often see the hostages' families asking the kidnappers to prove that the hostages are alive before they talk about the ransom because they don't want to find out that the hostages have been killed after the ransom is paid. When that happens, the kidnappers usually show a photo of the hostage holding the newspaper issued that day to prove that the hostage was still alive when the newspaper was published.

Here, the "newspaper issuing time" is equivalent to a timestamp.

In the digital world, timestamps prove that a specific file has existed at a particular time. Of course, the form is no longer a rubber stamp or a photo but a string of data used to represent time.

A widely used data form is the Unix timestamp, which refers to the total number of seconds from 00:00:00 on January 01, 1970, GMT until a certain moment.

For example, 3600 means 01:00:00 on January 1, 1970.

This timestamp is also used to mark the birth time of each Bitcoin block.

A block is born when a person figures out the answer to a mathematical puzzle designed by Satoshi Nakamoto, and the person mining the bloc is called a miner. The miners timestamp their mined blocks to record their birth time.

However, there may be errors in the time on these miners' watches, so their timestamps can't be completely synchronized. Bitcoin timestamps only need to be accurate to the hour.

Like other data recorded on the blockchain, the timestamp can't be doctored once registered on a blockchain.

Similar to the plot in a kidnapping movie, using a newspaper's release time as a timestamp is trustworthy because news can't be predicted in advance.

40 Block Height

The block height is the distance from a block to the first block. This height accurately describes the block's position on a blockchain, equivalent to giving the block a "coordinate."

It is similar to the road network in the U.S. Its interstate and intrastate highways are numbered with a fixed number pattern: odd numbers for north-south roads and even for west-east ones. The numbers increase from west

to east and south to north. Take Interstate 5 (I-5 in short), for example. It is the westernmost north-south highway in the U.S. Therefore, as long as a driver sees the numbers, he can quickly tell the highway's direction and the approximate bearings.

With the block height, the block's location can also be seen at a glance.

It should be noted that the calculation rule of block height doesn't start from 1. The height of the first block is recognized as 0, so the height of the 50th block is 49.

It is like Britons regarding the second instead of the first floor as the first floor.

41 SHA-256

SHA is short for Secure Hash Algorithm, a generic term for the hash function. SHA-256 refers to one of the algorithms in which the hash value has a fixed length of 256 bits in binary.

You may have returned your computer knowledge to your junior-high-school teacher. So, let me rekindle your memory a bit. Binary is a set of computer-counting methods. No matter whether the data you enter is Chinese characters, English, or numbers, the computer will use "0" and "1" to record it.

Suppose you are in a large library with a 300,000-word masterpiece titled One Hundred Years of Solitude in your hand. The so-called "hash"

refers to compressing these 300,000 words into a string of binary numbers, such as "0100110...." This number string corresponds to the original 300,000 words of information.

SHA-256 means that the compressed "0s" and "1s" total 256 bits. Therefore, this One Hundred Years of Solitude tome can be identified by combining two hundred and fifty-six "0s" or "1s."

Likewise, other books in the library can be compressed to 256 bits. Even with the same One Hundred Years of Solitude, different versions, publishers, and translations can have diverse "0" and "1" combination results due to subtle discrepancies in the original information. The length of 256 bits guarantees many possible combinations of "0s" and "1s."

Tx:12e4d
Tx:1045f
Tx:60ed4cf
Tx:6731e
Input:07e5
Tx:07c4e

Now, imagine that a mysterious library director comes on the scene, asking a group of people to add a few words to a page in the book *One Hundred Years of Solitude* so that the 256-bit binary number obtained after hashing the book can be smaller than the number he has given. Whoever can do it sooner will be rewarded.

You must have discovered by now that this game is similar to bitcoin mining. How many words should you add so that the compressed hash of *One Hundred Years of Solitude* is what the director wants precisely? It's full of chance.

42 Merkle Tree

In cryptographic applications, it is rare to directly hash a piece of data once and transmit it by deriving a single hash value. Because once the data is damaged during transmission, it is difficult to locate what minute part of the data is problematic.

The usual method is first to cut the data into many small data blocks, hash each small data block separately, and then hash together the hash values obtained from two adjacent small data blocks. If the data block is an odd number, a transaction is automatically copied, and after the data block becomes an even number, two-by-two hashing is performed. This process is repeated until the last hash value is generated.

Suppose a large data is cut into ten small data blocks by "hashing adjacent small data blocks once." Six hash values are obtained after the first hash and four after the second try. The hashing continues this way four times until the last hash value is obtained.

Each hash value is stored in this process, and the number of hash values generated decreases layer by layer, so the shape is like a tree with a lush canopy, and the entire data structure is called a Merkle tree.

The "last hash value" is called the Merkle root.

Did you notice it? According to the characteristics of the hash function, if two data have the same Merkle root, the two data must be precisely the same.

If the Merkle tree roots of the two data are different, you can quickly troubleshoot the problem by examining the hash values layer by layer. This method is often used in P2P networks and distributed systems.

Where the Bitcoin application is concerned, this Merkle tree data structure is used to record all transactions in a blockchain to check which transaction on the chain has been altered.

In short, this data structure is to hash the transactions in a block layer by layer to obtain a Merkle root, which is stored in this block's block header. Once a transaction in a block is changed, it will conflict with the Merkle root.

Finally, let's imagine such a game to further our understanding.

A teacher had 16 children sit in the first row, eight in the second row, four in the third, two in the fourth, and one in the fifth. Each child holds two small flags, one red and one blue, in hand.

The teacher asks that every two children in the front row correspond to one child in the back row. If the two children in the front row raise red flags, the corresponding children in the back row raise the flag of the same color. If the flags raised by the two children in the front row are one red and one blue,

SPV

or both blue, then the flag raised by the corresponding child in the back row must be blue.

The operation goes to the third, fourth, and fifth rows until the children in the fifth row raise their flags.

The teacher only told the 16 children in the first row to raise red flags. Now, he checks the colors of the flags raised by the 16 children in the fifth row. If they are holding blue flags up, one child must have made a mistake and raised the wrong one.

That is to say, without checking the entire process of each child raising their flags in each row, the teacher can quickly know whether there is an error in the process.

43 SPV

SPV is short for Simplified Payment Verification. As the name suggests, it is a relatively simple method for verifying payments. It is a Bitcoin-specific concept.

Let's first look at a situation in which you may need to verify a payment, that is, to verify a transaction.

Suppose you transfer a coin to someone, and he keeps claiming that he didn't receive it. Now, you are also confused: The transaction information you sent has been hashed and yielded a hash value called "Transaction ID," and you have the transaction's hash value in your hands. But you don't know whether other miners have linked the deal to a blockchain. So, you want to find a miner to ask about the situation.

It is like going to a faraway library to borrow a book, but you don't want to make the trip without getting the book. Therefore, you want to check if the book is available in the library. If so, where is it located there?

The only thing you can think of doing is searching for it in the online catalog, filling in the title and publisher, and getting the search result.

In the blockchain network, miners possess a complete ledger comparable to the "library retrieval system." To verify the existence of a transaction, you need to send your transaction ID to a nearby miner so that he can help you find the block where the transaction is located in the ledger.

The ideal situation is if your transaction is really on the chain, then the miner should give you a positive answer, and if it isn't, he will provide a negative response.

It sounds like the problem is solved. But remember, in a pure blockchain world, no one would assume a person is kindhearted for no reason. The Satoshi Nakamoto-designed blockchain network is always wary of the possibility of various evils. What if this miner you have never met happens to be a liar?

But you are unlikely to download a complete blockchain ledger to verify his words because it consumes too much hard disk capacity. At this point, you should appreciate the existence of SPV. The idea of this simple verification method is that you only need to download all the block headers to verify whether the miner has lied to you. The capacity of each Bitcoin block is 1 megabyte or 1048576 bytes, and the block header size is only 80 bytes, making your download task much more manageable.

We may as well call it the "block-head ledger." Each block header stores the Merkle root obtained by hashing all the transactions in a blockchain. The hash value you have acquired by hashing your and your neighbors' transactions is like a small "leaf" on this data tree. This hash value forms another "leaf" with the adjacent hash value.

You can ask the miners to provide the transaction ID of the transaction adjacent to yours and the hash values of this thread like stacked-up "leaves." Then, you calculate a Merkle root and compare it with the Merkle root in the "block-header ledger."

If the miner lied, claiming a transaction is non-existent on the chain. To deceive you, he must forge transaction records so that the Merkle root obtained after the transaction hash he provided is the same as the Merkle root stored in the "block-header ledger" you downloaded. However, based on hash characteristics, the changes in original data and hash value are irregular, so the possibility of piecing together a specific hash value is negligibly slight.

In other words, as long as you find two identical Merkle roots, it is almost impossible for a miner to lie. He must have located the transaction information.

44 Encryption

Encryption is a means of protecting information. It turns plaintext into ciphertext to prevent information from being intercepted and tampered with when transmitted in an insecure network.

The encryption algorithm is the specific method used for encryption.

For example, someone wants to send you a "HELLO BLOCKCHAIN" message now, and he moves each letter 6 bits backward in alphabetical order, turning the plaintext into the ciphertext of "NKRRU HRUIQINGOT." The message will most likely confuse you.

In this case, "move backward in the alphabet" is an encryption algorithm. But you obviously can't restore the plaintext just by knowing the algorithm alone because you must also know how many bits have been moved. It is like you only know a lock's manufacturer, but you can't open the lock without its key in your hand.

Let's return to the "HELLO BLOCKCHAIN" example. The number 6 is the key that opens the lock, called the "key." You must know both the

encryption algorithm and key to crack a ciphertext.

Since cryptocurrency transactions are also exposed to insecure network environments, the blockchain world is inseparable from encryption technology. Encryption algorithms and keys protect transaction information. The encrypted data is like a billiard ball on the table. You can only see its current position, but it is difficult to deduce where it starts, how many times it will be hit, and in what trajectory it will roll.

45 Symmetric-key Algorithm

The same key is used for encryption and decryption when encryption is realized using a symmetric-key algorithm.

Suppose you want to encrypt a file and transmit it to a partner. If you choose a symmetric-key algorithm, you must negotiate and agree upon a key with the other party in advance, which you and your partner will keep. You use this key to encrypt the file, and he will use it to decrypt it.

Suppose the other party is muddle-headed and accidentally loses his key or places it somewhere everyone can see. In that case, the document's confidentiality between you can't be guaranteed because the key you keep is also exposed. On the other hand, whether you tell the other party the key through an online social platform or write it down, put it in an envelope, and send it to him, others may see and copy it during the transmission process.

For example, you must have heard this boring tale: A princess and a knight fall in love at first sight. But the princess's royal parents are against their love affair. To hide it from them, the two youngsters communicate in secret.

The princess asked her maidservant to send a letter to the knight, saying that they would hide the location and time of their tryst in the first letter of the word heading each line of an "acrostic poem."

As long as the two write and read letters according to the agreed method, they will complete the encryption and decryption process. And the key was the rule of writing their letters in the first letter the maidservant sent.

The princess and the knight didn't expect a flaw in their secret agreement: If the king's cronies could bribe the maidservant and see the rule, the "key" between the young couple would be revealed.

Therefore, securely transmitting and storing symmetric keys is a significant issue.

46 Asymmetric-key Algorithm

Imagine you are so muddle-headed that you accidentally put your roommate's key in your pocket and bring it with you when you go on a business errand. Then, you think about mailing it back to him. Your roommate will undoubtedly want to throw a rotten tomato on your face when he sees you again. The reason is simple: The chance of the key being intercepted and used to open the room by a thief is too great.

The fiction describes a scenario similar to a symmetric-key algorithm. Let's continue the imagined story and think about how you will have the "key" safely sent back. Another invention, the asymmetric-key or public-key algorithm, could solve your problem.

With the application of the asymmetric-key algorithm, two different but paired keys are generated. One is privately kept and needs no transmission, so it is called a private key. The other, called the public key, is publicized and doesn't need to be kept secret.

The information encrypted with one of the keys can only be decrypted by the other paired key. So the public and private keys form a unique corresponding relationship.

Because of this unique corresponding relationship, the asymmetric-key algorithm firstly functions to verify the information sender's identity. For example, if you want to send a message now, encrypt it with asymmetric encryption and generate a private and public key. You keep the private key yourself, and the message recipient has received the public key that assuredly belongs to you. Since the public key and the private key are paired, as long as the other party can decrypt the message with your public key, he can confirm that the message is encrypted by your private key indeed. And it can prove that you are its sender.

The asymmetric-key algorithm can also be used for secure transmission. Suppose someone wants to send an encrypted message to you. You can generate a private and public key, send the latter to the other party, and ask him to encrypt his message with the key and send it to you. Only you can decrypt the message with your private key.

Now, let's look at a real case. An American named Frank wanted to encourage strangers to write about their secrets and mail them to him. He printed 3,000 postcards with his return address and distributed them to strangers on the streets of Washington, D.C.

The secrets can be regarded as information needing encryption, and their owners didn't want them to be publicized on the Internet. They only wanted to mail them to Frank himself. Putting the postcards with their secrets

into the public mailbox is comparable to using the public-key algorithm.

Only Frank has the key to the mailbox, so only he can read the secrets. This key is the private key.

47 Digital Signature

First, let us think about why we need signatures in real life. With a name signed at the end of a document and delivered, the recipient can confirm the signer's approval of the document's content. Second, anything falsified in the document can prove malicious because no one will sign their name beneath the doctored text.

Digital signatures probably play the same role in the digital world. However, unlike real-world signatures, digital signatures don't require a pen, nor is handwriting verified by a third-party agency.

The digital signature is an application of the asymmetric-key algorithm.

Let's review what we have discussed about the asymmetric-key algorithm. Two paired keys are generated when using this algorithm. One key is privately kept and needs no transmission, thus being called the private key. The other is publicized and doesn't need to be kept secret. It is thus called the public key.

A message encrypted with one of the keys can only be decrypted by the other key. So, the public and private keys form a unique corresponding relationship.

You might as well give free rein to your imagination and fancy a scenario to understand how digital signatures work. Now, you have time-traveled back to the Qing Dynasty, where you are a prince sent to the front. One of your buddies in contemporary times has become your royal father. For communication security, you generated a pair of keys, one public and the other private, before your departure. You kept the private key and gave the public one to your father. Urgent messages keep coming from the front, and you write a letter to the Qing court to ask for reinforcement. You demonstrate your incredible cryptographic skills to ensure that your message won't be intercepted and tampered with by the enemy on its way.

You hash the content of your letter first, and no matter how much you want to say, it is "compressed" into a short "digest."

Subsequently, you encrypt the digest as plaintext with your private key and get a digital signature. You attach the signature to the letter asking for reinforcement and send it to your royal father.

The process of your father verifying the digital signature is similar to decryption. He first decrypts the digital signature with the public key paired with your private key to get a digest. Then, he hashes the main body of your letter again to get another digest. If in comparison, the two digests agree, the letter is undoubtedly from you without being tampered with during its transmission. Your royal father happily sends troops to your aid.

In the blockchain network, correspondingly, you initiate a cryptocurrency transaction. The miners who act as bookkeepers must verify if you possess the cryptocurrency in this transaction. The method they use is to verify your digital signature.

Your royal father plays the role of the miner. Likewise, your transfer can take effect only when the miners have verified your digital signature.

48 Blind Signature

A school is electing a student association president. A teacher in charge uses secret ballots to make the process fair. Standing on the rostrum, he put a red box on the podium. You, as the students, write the name on small paper slips, fold them, and place them in the box.

The teacher can't see the candidate you picked. He only ticks off a form with the students' names of the same graduation year to ensure that you are in the year and eligible to vote and that you have voted.

This example of what happens daily in the real world shows the teacher endorsing the "legality" of a paper slip by ticking it without even knowing what is written on it. He only needs to make sure the voting process is appropriate. In this scenario, only you know for whom you have voted. The teacher sees your vote but doesn't know for which candidate you have cast your vote.

He is "blind," and your privacy is fully protected.

That is what blind signature does. You can understand it as the application of cryptography technology to a most simple secret ballot voting in real life. A voting system using blind signature technology involves two roles: the voter and the notary. Voters first package their votes with their identity information to generate a message. After disguising (blinding) the voting information, you hand it to a notary for his blind signature. In this way, the notary can notarize the authenticity of the voter's identity without knowing for whom he voted.

The blind signature had been used as a cryptographic technology before blockchain's birth. Today, many practitioners committed to expanding the application scope of blockchain also store voting information in blocks, turning electronic voting into an application experiment of the blockchain.

49 Ring Signature

As you already know, the feature of the blind signature ensures that the signee is unaware of the content of a sender's message, whereas its recipient may know who has signed it.

The characteristic of the ring signature is to ensure that the recipient doesn't know who the signee is. In other words, the entire signing process is completed anonymously.

You may revisit the example of time-traveling back to the Qing court when we discussed the digital signature. Suppose you are still the prince fighting in the front and responsible for the decision to get reinforcement. What will you do if you want your army beefed up while unwilling to let your father know you are the one who initiates the request with your signature?

The cunning ring signature comes to the scene to suit this situation.

Before you put your digital signature on the plea, you round up a random group of generals and soldiers to form a "signing group," including you. You signed this letter with your private key and all the others' public keys.

Your royal father can verify the signed information only with one of the public keys and confirm that the letter is neither forged nor doctored. But, interestingly, he will never know who in the "signature group" has signed it.

Since the generals and soldiers in the "signature group" have the same probability as you being the actual signer, the involvement of other signees conceals your identity as the signee.

As long as there are enough participants in this signature group, it becomes impossible to find the actual signees. It is the same as earthquake forecasting in real life. Suppose the forecast tells you there will be violent seismic movements in a vast land in the next 30 years. It is an utterly useless piece of information for you who what to know precisely when and where to evacuate.

Let's return to the scenario of cryptocurrency transactions. With a ring signature, you signed the transaction you had initiated with your private key and the public keys of a random group of participants as a temporary "signature group." When verifying the transaction, the miners see only the public keys of everyone in the group. Since there is no way to determine which public key is your real transaction initiator, the miners can by no means trace the specific source of the transfer.

If the ring signature is combined with other technologies, it can significantly increase the cost of tracing a fund's whereabouts. These characteristics coincide with cryptocurrency transactions that strongly advocate freedom and privacy.

50 Multi-signature

Have you ever gone through a project completion report? It is stamped with the signature seals of all the people involved in the construction: the supervisors, surveyors, designers, and contractors. In other words, the report is in effect only when these signatures appear simultaneously.

In the context of the blockchain network, multi-signature involves multiple participants in the joint management of a digital asset.

Where blockchain is concerned, the relationship between people and the needs around this relationship hasn't changed substantially, so you can understand that blockchain is always pursuing to reproduce multi-facet real life by technical means to the maximum degree.

Suppose you and your partners jointly establish a public digital asset account similar to a bank "joint account." Now, you want to initiate a transfer.

If it is an ordinary account, you only need to sign it with your private key and leave it to the miners in the network to use the matching public key to verify the identity. In a public account using multi-signature technology, which and how many participants co-sign the transaction are pre-determined to make it effective. Therefore, the signees must reach the pre-agreed number after you initiate one before it can take effect.

Interestingly, even alone, you can create a multi-signature account and use its features to solve some practical problems.

For example, if you are incredibly forgetful, you can generate a public and private key. It is agreed that only one of the private key signatures is required to use the money after the account is created. That way, you don't have to be heartbroken about forgetting one of your private keys. After all, losing your private key is the same as losing your digital asset. Many panicky and careless people worldwide have to get a "hypnotist" to help them recall their passwords. The multi-signature reduces the chance of that tragedy happening to you.

Let's assume you are exceedingly cautious. You can pre-agree that the money can be used when signed with two private keys simultaneously. What you guard against isn't your carelessness but the elusive hackers. You don't have to worry about your private key being stolen anymore.

51 Digital Certificate

Whenever you drag your luggage, carry your boarding pass, stride to the airport security checkpoint, and hand over your passport through a window, have you ever thought about why you need this identification in the real world?

A passport is a pass to verify your identity, with which you can travel worldwide. It is a document that proves you are "who you are." In a sense, the digital certificate is your "passport" in the blockchain network.

Let's look at the scenarios in which this "passport" will work.

Suppose you want to send a friend a message that needs to be kept secret. You can have him generate a public and private key uniquely paired, ask him for the public key, encrypt the message with it, and send it to him. Since only the private key he keeps can decrypt the message, the message transmission is theoretically guaranteed to be secure.

However, a devastating bomb may have been planted. What if your friend's public key is intercepted by a hooligan who replaces it with another public key when your friend first sent the original to you? A tragedy unfolds: you may use the hooligan's fake key to encrypt the message without knowing it, while he can use his private key to decrypt it. He can even communicate with you, pretending to be your friend.

Don't you think you have become a miserable wretch being kept in the dark in this story?

This tragedy could have been avoided if the friend had initially sent you the public key through a digital certificate. He could have submitted the information "My public key is..." to the digital-certificate-verifying CA (short for Certificate Authority). After the verification, the institute will issue him a certificate with the following information: the certificate's owner, the public key, the certificate's validity period, and the certificate's issuer. It looks like the pages of a genuine passport, right?

The CA will encrypt the information with its private key to keep it from being tampered with and prove that it is the original issuer of the certificate. What it does is attach a digital signature to the end of the certifying information to form a complete digital certificate.

Now, everything is ready at long last.

The friend sends you this digital certificate, and you can decrypt it with the public key released by the CA to see his public key. A hacker can do nothing malicious about the certificate, even if he intercepts it during its transmission. He may be able to decrypt the certificate. But, without the CA's private key, he can't tamper with and re-encrypt it before sending it out. Then, you won't fall victim to a lie.

It is worth mentioning that the CA is centralized, so in the blockchain network, digital certificates are mainly used by some consortium blockchain participants to prove their identities when communicating.

52 Wallet

Now, please put your hand in your pants pocket and take out your wallet. Don't you find some banknotes, coins, and credit cards whose passwords you know? Obviously, a wallet is a storage of your funds. You must take your money out and place the changes back into it when you pay.

In contrast, invisible and intangible, a cryptocurrency wallet is but a piece of software. But, similar to the physical wallet, its primary function is also to help people "take out" and "put back" their funds.

There is one stark difference: A cryptocurrency wallet does not hold a digital asset but a key. A true digital asset is the data stored in the blockchain ledger. People verify their identity and confirm the ownership of their digital assets using this key.

In real life, wallets are generally not locked, and you don't need a password when you take your money out of it. However, the cryptocurrency wallet with which you access your digital assets must be protected by a key. Those who don't know the key can't use the cryptocurrency associated with the wallet.

Although you may equate the key with the transfer password in your daily life, the intriguing thing is that this key isn't typed out on the keyboard. The wallet software randomly generates a long string of jumbled numbers and letters.

Cryptocurrency wallets operate based on the principle of asymmetric-key algorithm, that is, public- and private-key cryptography. And the wallet generates a pair of public and private keys. This random password that only the wallet owner can see is referred to as the private key.

As explained in the asymmetric-key algorithm section, the encryption process produces a public key, simultaneously in addition to a private one. The public and private keys enjoy a unique corresponding relationship. Therefore, only a private key can decrypt the information encrypted by a public key.

When a person initiates a "transfer" to you, the wallet's public key will generate an "address" where the money will be transferred. When he transfers the cryptocurrency into the wallet through this "address," only you who have the private key can access it.

Did you notice that once you lose your private key, you lose your digital assets forever?

The wallet keeps your digital assets; the essence is to generate and keep your private key. In addition to the most mainstream Bitcoin and Ethereum wallets, more and more cryptocurrencies have released theirs.

You can think of a wallet as a small box in your home where you keep all your keys. For convenience, you box all the keys to the cabinet and drawers in your house, and when you need to open a drawer, you take out the corresponding key from the box.

The inconspicuous little box plays an important role and is usually kept hidden because if a thief steals the key, the money in the drawer corresponding to the key is in jeopardy.

However, if you are new to cryptocurrencies, you may have doubts: When I buy a specific currency through an exchange, isn't it just a matter of logging in to the exchange account to check my assets? Where do I use the cryptocurrency wallet, then?

In this case, the private key of your cryptocurrency is stored in the exchange's "big safe."

Those who don't trust the exchange's security find it necessary to transfer the private key to a wallet developed by a third party. This wallet software is installed in their trusted computer and network environment.

Some coin holders don't even trust offline computers. They like to copy their private key on a note and deposit it in a physical safe themselves. Having no confidence in any institutions, they can be called extreme believers in decentralization.

53 Hot Wallet

In the financial world, funds float quickly, seeking short-term profits worldwide. They are called hot money. "Hot" refers to a feature with higher liquidity and more frequent activities, so "hot wallet" can be accessed and interacted with online.

You've already learned from the "wallet" section that it refers to software that produces and keeps a private key, which declares your digital asset ownership.

A hot wallet can store the private key locally on a device or a company server connectable to the Internet.

Take the wallet, for example. You can download wallet software to your mobile phone or computer that you use online to conduct cryptocurrency transactions.

When you use it for the first time, the software will let you know your private key, which will be installed on your phone or computer. In this case, you must avoid losing it from your device. So, you back up the private key. However, it doesn't eliminate the possibility of hackers breaking into your device and stealing it.

But you can use the hot wallet on a web browser without downloading any software.

In this case, your private key is stored on the server of the wallet-developing company, and the browser is just an interface for you to trade and view addresses and balances.

These servers tend to have better anti-theft measures than the local devices where you keep your private key. When you change your computer or mobile phone, you don't have to import the private key again. Instead, you only need to find a place with an internet connection, open a browser, and log into your wallet like a website.

But the hot wallet is not entirely safe. On the one hand, there is still the probability of being stolen by hackers. On the other, some hot wallet developers may act like thieves themselves.

However, the hot wallet's advantage is precisely its connectivity to the network. It is very convenient to conduct transactions using a hot wallet, and the transactions you initiate can be transmitted directly via the web.

Online hot wallet is like storing money on Alipay, WeChat, or a bank card. f you choose not to connect to the Internet, you must return home and take out the banknotes from under the pillow before spending them, which is very troublesome. The merit of doing so is keeping you from being defrauded of your account number. It also prevents your bank card from being stolen and duplicated.

54 Cold Wallet

The "cold wallet" concept is relative to the "hot wallet," and the two share standard features. Now, you can also roughly understand the characteristics of the cold wallet through the "Cold War" concept.

The Cold War was a state of confrontation and stalemate. At that time, the United States and the Soviet Union did not fire hot shots at each other. Used offline, the cold wallet is isolated from everything on the network without directly interacting with anything else.

The wallet has two functions: 1) producing and storing the private key representing your identity and 2) initiating a transaction. The transaction can only take effect when someone in the blockchain network verifies your private key and determines that you're the digital asset owner. Obviously, transactions must be initiated online.

Strictly speaking, it shouldn't be called the cold wallet because it's offline. It doesn't have the function of initiating cryptocurrency transactions

anymore. Therefore, it isn't a wallet in the true sense. It only functions to produce and store the private key for digital assets.

Because of this, it is referred to as "cold storage" in many sources abroad.

Suppose you pull a dust-covered old computer without a Wi-Fi card or a broken mobile phone with a malfunctioned network module from your storage attic. In that case, you can use them for a better purpose: your cold wallet only to record the long string of numbers and letters that constitute your private key.

Their defects are precisely what a cold wallet needs because it relies on an offline mode to generate and keep private keys. You'll never need to connect them to the Internet when you use them later. You'll keep hackers at bay by doing so.

The cold wallet many people choose is a mere piece of fade-resistant paper. With full respect, they neatly pen the private key on it. Some "wealthy" people keep the slip in a safe.

The situation is like what a celebrity finds himself in: He has recorded a video of his family with the residence soon to evacuate and fears that they might be flesh-searched by the offline and online media. He must give up the idea of storing the video in a cloud or portable memory to protect his family's privacy.

He must isolate the video from the online network to ensure his family's privacy isn't stolen. For example, he can stow the video camera with the video in a drawer away from public view.

The drawback of this method is that he must stay at home to view the video recording of his family's precious memory at the sacrifice of the convenience of watching it anywhere, anytime.

Doesn't it sound like a hassle to use a cold wallet? The good news is that many kinds of wallet software considerately have the dual function of cold and hot wallets.

It doesn't work anymore if you only jot the cold key down on paper. You must have two computers or mobile phones, one offline and the other online, and download the same software with the above-mentioned dual function to each computer or phone.

You will store your private key on the offline device and use the device connected to the Internet to initiate transactions. After the initiation, a QR code will be automatically produced containing the transaction information. You will scan the QR code with the offline device and add your private key. Then, the Internet-connected device can transmit the transaction to the blockchain network.

Of course, if the computer or mobile phone you use for cold storage is damaged, you may still lose the private key for your digital assets.

The convenience of transactions will suffer with the cold wallet. Therefore, it is more suitable for situations where digital assets are enormous, security requirements are high, and transactions are infrequent.

Some exchanges store most of the private keys for digital assets in cold storage while making a small part of the assets available to users.

55 Mnemonic Phrase

Probably very few people in the world can recall their private keys right away. They're random combinations of numbers and letters, after all.

However, the cost of forgetting private keys is enormous, for you'll permanently lose the opportunity to prove to the blockchain network that you're the owner of a specific digital asset.

You may make a clerical error even if you write your private key down, like copying "01" into "00" or mixing the number "0" with the letter "O." You'll find it hard to recognize it over time.

For that reason, the mnemonic phrase was born to help people memorize private keys.

A mnemonic phrase is generally an arranged sequence of 12 to 24 English words, and the wallet software will show you what it is.

It can be seen as another form of the private key. The publication of the mnemonic phrase will expose your private key. Therefore, taking good care of it is as essential as safekeeping the private key.

But it is easier to remember because the long string of numbers and letters in a private key becomes meaningful words such as "apple" and "cat." Of course, some locally produced software also introduced local lexicons like Chinese.

It doesn't sacrifice the private key's security because only those who can guess the words and enter them in the intended order will know your private key.

Mnemonic phrases are deemed impossible due to the immense size of their lexicons. By the way, the mnemonic phrase lexicon isn't Satoshi Nakamoto's masterpiece. Enthusiasts of Bitcoin's open-source community have jointly created it.

The mnemonic phrase is reminiscent of the famous musical The Sound of Music. People invent various magical methods to facilitate their memory, transforming abstract and intangible knowledge into a realistic picture, a definitive text, or even a song.

In *The Sound of Music*, governess Maria finds that Captain Georg von Trapp's children have difficulty memorizing the seemingly irregular Do, Re, Mi, Fa, So, La, T. notes. Therefore, while playing her guitar, she composes a Do-Re-Mi song in a breeze-filled valley: "Do, a deer, a female deer / Re, a drop of golden sun...."

She associates "Do" with the English word "doe." The children quickly memorize the seven notes with the help of a catchy melody and lively lyrics.

56 Nodes

With the click of a finger, you've launched a cryptocurrency exchange website and tentatively bought an encrypted coin, thus striking a deal. You're now called a participant in the blockchain network. But I'm afraid you would be too imaginative if you immediately claimed to be a "node."

In fact, the concept of "participant" is more generic than "node." Nodes may be all over the world and have, together, formed an immense blockchain network. But only a point with encrypted currency transmitted to a wallet that keeps the private key can be referred to as a node.

However, nodes vary from one another, and the criterion for judging the difference is whether all the data on a blockchain has been downloaded. In other words, it depends on whether this node stores the complete blockchain ledger locally. A node that has downloaded all the blockchain data and can be continuously synchronized to the latest block is called a "full node."

The full nodes can independently verify each received transaction and determine whether the originator of the transaction has sufficient balance to spend. Meanwhile, they're also responsible for putting verified transactions into new blocks.

A full node is essentially the creator and maintainer of the blockchain. Decentralization is possible thanks to their existence. The number of full nodes also affects the stability of the entire blockchain network.

Take the Bitcoin blockchain, for example. All the miners involved in mining are the full node.

Of course, most nodes are "light nodes" because full nodes must sacrifice storage space to accommodate the transaction ledge with its pages multiplying indefinitely. By the end of February 2020, the total Bitcoin data size had reached around 265GB.

The light node downloads only the data in all the block headers. The size of the block headers was only 47MB during the same period. It's indeed light compared with the storage burden of the full node. Many wallets that can initiate transfer transactions for you are light nodes, so you who possess cryptocurrency in your wallet can also call yourself a light node.

However, many functions have been omitted from the light node compared with the full node. A light node can't verify a transaction since it doesn't have a complete ledger. On the contrary, it must use the information provided by the full node to query whether a transaction has been added to a blockchain.

We can find real-life examples of the relationship between the full node and the light node. You can treat bank branches as nodes. Some are mini-branches with only ATMs, where you can only transfer money or check the balance in their glassed booths. You must travel to a larger branch when conducting a transaction that calls for bank tellers' review because only they have the function of providing more complex services, such as checking up on your funds.

57 UTXO

The full name of UTXO is Unspent Transaction Output. It's a set of accounting methods designed by Satoshi Nakamoto for Bitcoin. In real life, when someone asks you how much money you have in your bank account, you only need to click on your online banking website and glance at the balance. The "account balance" is your "unspent transaction."

The same is true for offline fiat currency transactions. Today, you received a salary of 100 yuan from your money-pinching boss and spent 50 yuan for a meal. In the evening, the boss mercifully gave you an extra 20 yuan as a subsidy for working in high temperatures. You immediately purchased a ten-yuan package of cigarettes with the 20-yuan banknote and got a ten-yuan banknote change.

It's easy for you to check your balance now. You don't have to figure out where you got all your money. You have a 50-yuan banknote and a 10-yuan banknote in your pocket, with a sum of 60 yuan. If you want to buy a book worth 60 yuan the following day, you only need to ensure you have enough funds in your pocket.

Let's apply this example to the Bitcoin network, where each of your expenditures is treated as an "output." Using the UTXO model, we can say the number of banknotes in your pocket is equivalent to a UTXO record. When you want to spend 50 yuan on a meal, the miner responsible for bookkeeping will check your account to see if you have enough UTXOs to

make up the 50 yuan. Now that he has found a 100-yuan UTXO unspent in your account, your transaction request is judged to be legitimate.

When you spent 50 yuan in a restaurant, two UTXO records were generated. One is the record of 100 yuan you used to buy the meal, and the other is the record of the 50 yuan change you received. Incidentally, it's worth noting that the original UTXO record will be invalid once you make a purchase with all your money. So, after receiving the high-temperature subsidy, you have only two UTXO records in your account, one being the 10-yuan banknote and the other the 50-yuan banknote. When you want to spend 60 yuan on a book that will help you upgrade your knowledge or skills, the bookkeeping miner only needs to check the UTXO in your account to see if you have the 60 yuan.

Why did Satoshi Nakamoto design such a mechanism for Bitcoin bookkeeping? Why didn't he create a model for adding and subtracting account balances like a bank, as Ethereum and some other cryptocurrencies do?

In the above transaction process, you'll find that if you use the account balance model, you can only see a final deposited figure but not all the transactions circulating before this balance. If we use the UTXO record model, we'll find that each expenditure will void the original UTXO record and generate a brand-new UTXO. Both the canceled-out and newly generated records are stored in a block. Therefore, the source of each UTXO can be traced.

On the other hand, in the UTXO mode, you can activate a different address every time you receive coins others have transferred to you. When you want to spend the coins, the bookkeeping miner can only check if you have the UTXO of sufficient funds on the address where the coins are located. In other words, even if this address were monitored one day, the addresses you use to accept different currencies would still be hidden under the iceberg. Of course, you may ask, with the account balance model, can't this be achieved by opening different accounts? But in fact, if you open additional accounts, you need to memorize extra private keys. But all UTXO addresses are associated with the same private key.

PART

4

External Interest

58 51% Attack

Mining is a competition. The difference in hashing power directly affects the probability of successful mining. What will happen if the power is too concentrated?

At a company's shareholders' general meeting, the shareholder who owns more than 50% of the shares is called the "controlling shareholder," with the vetoing right. Even if other shareholders favor a resolution, it cannot be passed as long as he votes against it.

Similarly, if a real "Lord Voldemort" were in control of most of the computing power of the entire blockchain network, he would be given the same all-powerful privilege.

Suppose, unfortunately, this "Lord Voldemort" is a malicious mining pool, or there is a group of villains with 51% of the hashing power on the entire blockchain network ganging up to do evil. In that case, the attack they launch would be called the "51% attack."

The principle of the 51% attack is related to a mechanism of the Bitcoin network.

After miner A mines a new block, he'll broadcast it to the entire network, but there is a delay in the broadcasting. Sometimes, miner B may also have mined a block. He then spreads the news to other miners without receiving miner A's broadcast in time.

Thus, two branches have emerged in the blockchain network.

A set of recognized "choice mechanisms" has been established for the entire network in response to this situation. According to the mechanisms, only one chain is recognized: The branch followed by the most blocks will be retained, and all the blocks on the other branch will be invalidated.

The 51% attack takes advantage of this mechanism. An attacker can spend the same number of bitcoins over and over again.

The attacker conducts the transaction with bitcoins first, and this transaction information will be connected to the latest block on the blockchain according to the accounting principles. Then, he quickly adds new blocks after the block preceding the one that recorded the transaction. He can successfully build the longest chain if he adds blocks fast enough.

Since the Bitcoin network always recognizes the longest chain only, the original chain will be revoked instead. The block that records this attacker's transaction information will also be invalidated, and the bitcoins he has previously transferred will be back in his hands.

You have discovered that the premise of a successful attack depends on the speed with which the attacker builds branches. According to probabilistic calculations, when someone has 51% of the entire network's computing power and maintains it for a certain period, his attack is bound to succeed. When someone has 30% of the whole network's computing power, his attack has a certain chance of success.

59 Double-spending

Double-spending means the same digital token is spent more than once.

There's no double-spending problem when cash is used in transactions because a transfer is completed when a certain amount of money is paid. It wouldn't be the same money even if the payer counterfeited banknotes with the same serial numbers and spent them afterward.

In the blockchain network, however, digital assets are traded, which is essentially the transfer of virtual information. Therefore, there is the possibility that the same assets are doubly spent.

A 51% attack can make double-spending possible.

In the tortoise-hare race, if the tortoise-chasing hare runs 100 times faster than the tortoise without dozing off, it will eventually catch up with the tortoise even if it lags far behind.

In the same way, an attacker with more than 51% of the entire network's computing power can add blocks faster than ordinary miners so that he can create a recognized longest chain more quickly.

According to the principle of "51% attack" introduced earlier, the attacker can return the spent digital assets to his account.

It's like a cunning person using a payphone and has threaded a thin string through the coin. He can pull the coin out after finishing the phone call to void the transaction. He can then make countless calls in the same way.

Besides, there is a time lapse between the generation of a transaction record and its connection to a blockchain. Double-spending can "make trouble" by taking advantage of this "time difference."

Take Bitcoin as an example. Mr. A bought bread from Ms. B with a bitcoin. He instantly initiated another transaction with the same coin and purchased coffee from Mr. C before a miner connected Mr. A's initial transaction to a blockchain. One of the transactions might not have been verified by the miner in time, but Mr. A successfully obtained the bread and coffee.

When fully aware of the "time difference," you'll find that you must wait until a transaction is confirmed multiple times to avoid this double-spending.

When a transaction record is inserted into the block and added to its end, we say it has received a confirmation. If a new block follows this one, it is said to have received two confirmations, and so on.

Double-spending occurs because the payee delivers the goods to the payer with zero transaction confirmation. Multiple confirmations are the premise of ensuring secure transactions.

60 Replay Attack

When you can't sleep at night, you may press the loop button of your music player app to let a lullaby replay constantly. Replay means playing a melody over and over.

In the blockchain network, a replay attack refers to an act of network fraud by repeatedly broadcasting the same transaction message.

A replay attack generally happens in two scenarios: The first occurs between the hard-fork-created new chain and the original chain. Let's take Bitcoin's hard fork as an example.

Suppose you have a bitcoin in your wallet. One day, a group of angry people suddenly "hard forked" a new chain issuing the cryptocurrency "Bitcoin Cash." You are pleasantly surprised to find one more Bitcoin Cash coin added to the coin in your wallet though you've never bought the cash. You wonder why you're blessed with such a windfall.

That is because before the hard forking transpired, everyone had maintained the same transaction ledger. But after that, Bitcoin Cash may have started keeping an account book of its own, but it still shares all the transaction data before the hard fork.

In other words, if Bitcoin Cash miners need to verify an instance of its transaction, they must also trace it back to a block on the Bitcoin network.

Similarly, from the perspective of the complete data chain of Bitcoin Cash, all Bitcoin transactions before the hard fork are Bitcoin Cash transactions. Therefore, a bitcoin in your account is equivalent to a Bitcoin Cash coin. With the front-end technical support of the wallet or exchange, you can see the two tokens in your possession.

Because the two chains share the same ledger before the fork, the bitcoin in your wallet and the Bitcoin Cash windfall are replicas from a code point of view. Perpetrators of replay attacks can take advantage of this phenomenon.

After the hard fork, you want to transfer this Bitcoin Cash coin but are unwilling to do the same with your bitcoin. The perpetrator can broadcast the transaction information you published on the Bitcoin Cash network to the Bitcoin network. Since the addresses, keys, and transaction formats of the two coins are the same, bitcoin miners will verify that the transaction is legitimate. You wanted to transfer a Bitcoin Cash coin, but you lost a bitcoin at the same time due to a replay attack.

Another replay attack occurs inside a blockchain.

When I introduced the UTXO accounting mechanism, I mentioned that if a person transfers a bitcoin to you, the UTXO generated by the bitcoin he received in the past will be invalid. Every spent bitcoin will generate a brand new UTXO, so each bitcoin can only be spent once.

It is necessary to prevent replay attacks because some cryptocurrencies, like Ethereum, do not use the UTXO mechanism.

Without technical precautions, perpetrators can use replay attacks to gain horrific benefits on Ethereum.

When you remit 2,000 yuan to a friend at a bank counter, you must fill in a remittance form. The teller will deduct the money from your account after verifying the legality of your transaction. The replay attack in Ethereum is similar to someone copying your remittance form and transferring one sum after another of your funds until depleting your balance.

The same goes for the Ethereum network. If there are no security measures against replay attacks, a perpetrator can repeatedly broadcast the information that you initiated the transaction, and the miners will verify it. As long as the balance in your account is sufficient, your coins will become his.

You can also imagine by analogy that a store has issued a limited number of QR code coupons, and users can enjoy the discount by showing the QR code in the store. But the store can't identify whether a coupon has been scanned. From time to time, someone can present the same coupon repeatedly by exploiting this loophole. As a result, the store will suffer.

- **Related vocabulary**

  68. Hard Fork

61 Replay Attack Protection

You already know that a replay attack means that the perpetrator repeatedly broadcasts transaction information so that the transferor's assets flow out continuously. Protection against replay attacks is a protection measure taken to prevent this kind of attack.

The key to preventing the risk of a replay attack after a blockchain's hard fork is making the transformation information on one chain invalid on the

other. Let's return to the previous example. When you initiate a request to transfer a Bitcoin Cash coin, the Bitcoin network must fully recognize that the request to transfer a bitcoin is illegal.

You can protect against replay attacks in many ways. For example, you can change how the new chain is signed after the fork or alter the transaction format.

Take the development team of Bitcoin Cash as an example. It adds a particular identifier to the transaction format. When you initiate a Bitcoin Cash transaction, the Bitcoin network can recognize this identifier, and all identified dealings will be considered invalid in the Bitcoin network.

Conversely, when you initiate a Bitcoin transaction, the Bitcoin Cash network will reject you because you lack this identifier.

However, some development teams did not set up replay attack protection on newly forked chains, such as the SegWit2x that vanished halfway through its development. In fact, this project finally lost extensive computing power support, related to the lack of replay attack protection. No one wants to take risks in an ecosystem with obvious security vulnerabilities.

Of course, there are other strategies to deal with this situation. It requires a third party, such as an exchange or a wallet service provider, to protect users from the threat of replay attacks.

There are two general protection methods to protect against replay attacks like the one that plagues Ethereum.

One method is to place a timestamp on the transaction information, which is only valid when verified within a specific period after being timestamped. This way, a transaction will still be rejected even if its information is repeatedly broadcast because the time has expired.

It's like exchanging gifts with vouchers in our daily life; some of the coupons have unique serial numbers. The number becomes valid in the system's record when a gift is redeemed.

If a speculator duplicates a voucher and exchanges gifts with it, he can only get a reply from the staff that "this voucher has been redeemed." It is equivalent to setting up replay attack protection.

62 Sybil Attack

In 1973, a woman from Minnesota was suddenly known to more than 7 million readers. In her best-selling book Sybil, an eponymic woman Sybil is said to be able to split into 16 different personalities. A distinct personality awakens from her body in each fit of amnesia.

This split personality can be compared to "forging multiple identities through a single node to carry out network fraud." This plot is called a Sybil attack.

By launching a Sybil attack against a blockchain, the perpetrator can manipulate decisions on the chain to varying degrees.

Remember the consensus mechanism PBFT we introduced earlier? If more than one-third of the nodes in the system are malicious, the system will crash. Therefore, as long as the perpetrator forges enough fake nodes, it is possible to make it the consensus of other nodes through broadcasting.

Sybil attacks are initiated on peer-to-peer networks. The so-called peer-to-peer network means that the nodes in this network are "equal to all beings," and there is no authoritative node. You can compare it to such a scoring activity: it is stipulated that the evaluation results are determined by each participant scoring together on the network, and each person can only score once, and the scoring weights are the same.

You can imagine the result if a perpetrator has registered multiple IDs and used diverse identities to give high marks to the same work and low scores to all others. When the false identities reach a certain number, they will seriously impact the scoring.

However, the PoW consensus mechanism adopted by Bitcoin is naturally immune to Sybil attacks. That is because the rules formulated by PoW are to reward the most diligent miners in mining, which means the greater the hashing power there is, the higher probability of successful mining a miner will have. In the final analysis, the physical entity of the miner determines the right to have the final say on the chain. Therefore, even if you intend to forge multiple virtual identities, it isn't easy to construct numerous matching rigs out of thin air.

- **Related vocabulary**

  32. PoW

  36. PBFT

63 Dusting Attack

The dust suspended in the air may cause respiratory discomfort. The "dust" in the blockchain network refers explicitly to many small transactions that look like bits of "junk," causing pain to the entire transaction network.

Malicious miners can use this attack to disrupt a competitor's network.

The "junk" transactions they initiate are numerous and as meaningless as dust, whose sole purpose is to "make trouble" for the competitors.

As you already know, the capacity of each block on a blockchain is limited, limiting the transactions it can accommodate. In time, many transactions not inserted into the blocks must float in the network to wait for their turn. Dust transactions can worsen the network's congestion and make the timely processing of genuine transactions difficult.

It's like a malicious person already jealous of the competing store next door. One day, he takes a piggy bank filled with one-cent coins to the store to buy something worth a few hundred yuan, flabbergasting the store's cashier, who has to waste the store's service resources on counting the coins. She feels helpless even if a long customer queue is lining up for her service behind this malicious person.

There is also a dusting attack against Bitcoin.

Suppose you have a total of 500 bitcoins stored in ten different addresses, and one of the addresses holds 399 bitcoins that are not used very much. Someone "preying" on victims on the open Bitcoin network sees a significant sum of bitcoins on the specific address without knowing you yet.

He subsequently sends a dust transaction for 0.00001 bitcoin to this address. You miss the change to your total amount of bitcoins in time due to the tiny amount.

Remember how Bitcoin uses the UTXO model for bookkeeping? Several unique and non-renewable UTXO records will be created every time you make or receive a payment. So when this person transfers 0.00001 bitcoins, a UTXO associated with your specific address is created.

One day, when you transfer a bitcoin to a charity, the miners on the blockchain network will check whether you have sufficient bitcoins. They will go through all your addresses to find out if you have the UTXO of this bitcoin to donate. There is a certain probability for the 0.00001 bitcoin to produce this UTXO of a bitcoin by combining itself with other bitcoins. This UTXO will eventually be transferred to the address of the charity.

As you're congratulating yourself on doing a good deed, you're unaware of a pair of eyes "watching" your address being dusting-attacked. Your multiple addresses are exposed when the 0.00001 bitcoin and the bitcoins from several of your other addresses form the same transaction record and are plugged into blocks by miners to connect to the network.

Now, the "peeper" smirks because every bitcoin's spending record, sources, and destinations are transparent and traceable on the blockchain.

He can track and trace the history of your transaction information in these addresses and analyze some of your behavioral habits.

For example, you have used one of these addresses in some exchanges, which require you to upload your real-world identity information during registration. This way, the perpetrator can single out you, the owner of the 500 bitcoins, from so many people on the network. Your identity on the blockchain network is no longer a secret.

Another example is that he can also learn about your life by tracing a bitcoin transfer to a brick-and-mortar store you have made.

The person launching a dusting attack may be an extorter or a law enforcer tracking stolen money. Their purpose is to unmask you in cyberspace through such an attack. Some wallets provide reminder services, alerting you to "a small suspicious transaction," trying to stop the attack from happening and maintain the privacy of Bitcoin transactions.

- **Related vocabulary**

  57. UTXO

64 DDoS Attack

You can roughly understand the DDoS attack from the incidents of "spamming" Baidu or "spommenting" an online forum.

You may have known this incident: A movie star offended a particular

group of people, who then ganged up to visit the star's online forum simultaneously and post their comments at the speed of a few dozen per second. Since the mass posting was so fast that it exceeded the rate of the forum's owner manually deleting the comments, the forum was inundated and paralyzed, preventing other people from posting their regular comments.

The story roughly outlines how a DDoS attack works. It is an assault involving a large number of mining rigs that take up too many service resources by initiating reasonable service requests to the service provider and eventually collapse the service system.

You can now imagine a restaurant that seats 100 people at a time. Competitors on the same street hired 500 bullies to flock to the restaurant pretending to be regular diners. The bullies would neither place orders nor leave, causing the restaurant to fill up and keeping the owner from serving real diners.

The malicious competitor can be considered to launch a DDoS attack on the restaurant, exhausting its spatial resources and ultimately impeding its regular operation.

The difference between a rig and an online forum "mob" or a restaurant despot is that the former is likely to be "innocent," whereas the latter is primarily voluntary.

For example, some hackers bundle malware in the apps you download or send phishing messages to your email. Then, you'll inadvertently access a server, having your device "hijacked" by the hackers. They use this plot to control many computers and attack a target simultaneously.

The DDoS attack has hit cryptocurrency exchanges the hardest in recent years. Sometimes, a rising price curve causes those otherwise influential people to find it hard to buy bitcoins at the right time. They then hire some hackers to attack the websites and apps of the exchanges so that their customers can't log in and conduct legitimate transactions. The hacking will result in plummeting transaction volume and falling cryptocurrency prices. The competition for survival in global exchanges is exceptionally fierce. Therefore, some exchanges will hire hackers to attack their competitors' platforms, causing them to lose many customers because they fear their assets' safety is jeopardized.

65 Extortion

In May 2019, a smokeless attack occurred in Baltimore, east of the United States. The screens of the municipal government computers were suddenly locked. Then a rude statement popped up, demanding the government to "ransom" the seized computers and free the system back up with bitcoins.

"We won't talk more. All we know is MONEY! Hurry up! Tik Tak, Tik Tak, Tik Tak!" Knowing that demanding a bitcoin ransom would give them more sanctuary, this group of fanatics made this audacious statement.

Have you ever played the "whack-a-mole" game at the playground? Bitcoin ransomware "moles" have popped out of every "hole" in the world nonstop. In fact, if you search for recent-year news about ransomware, you'll find that Bitcoin has become increasingly potent.

Crazy hackers generally send untraceable emails with the threat, "We have the proof of your infidelity" or "We've taken over all your computers." They attach a guide for paying a ransom with bitcoins to the end of the emails.

In old-fashioned extortion cases, crazy perpetrators would always inadvertently leave some clues. For example, you must have seen such TV footage that police officers lay in wait by a trash can where the agreed ransom money would be dropped. Or you may have heard that some perpetrators unwittingly exposed their identities while asking for online money transfers.

Bitcoin, however, increases the ransom value and provides an ideal way of extortion. Criminals can change Bitcoin addresses at will because they are mere strings of random and untraceable letters and numbers. It's less effective and more complicated to catch the perpetrators with the dusting attack protection methods we've covered earlier.

Of course, those crazy hackers who gave the Baltimore municipal administrators such a headache didn't send any emails. Instead, they used the Bitcoin ransomware to launch the attack to the extreme.

The Bitcoin ransomware encrypts almost all kinds of files on your computer, making them impossible to launch normally and popping up a ransomware dialog window. Baltimore adamantly refused to pay the ransom. The cost was that citizens could not pay utility bills, visit government websites, or buy and sell houses in the following few weeks. It cost the municipal government tens of thousands of dollars to decrypt and repair the entire "kidnapped" system.

In May 2017, large-scale ransomware attacks broke out widely by exploiting the vulnerabilities in the Windows operating system. In just a few days, more than 200,000 computers in more than 150 countries were compromised, and many people and organizations had to deposit bitcoins in the addresses provided by the hackers.

The difficulty in tracking Bitcoin transactions has become these perpetrators' bargaining chip in their dirty dealings, such as illegally purchasing firearms. Law enforcement officers worldwide are facing a severe technical challenge.

Evil will never end as long as human nature is vicious. But technology itself should be innocent.

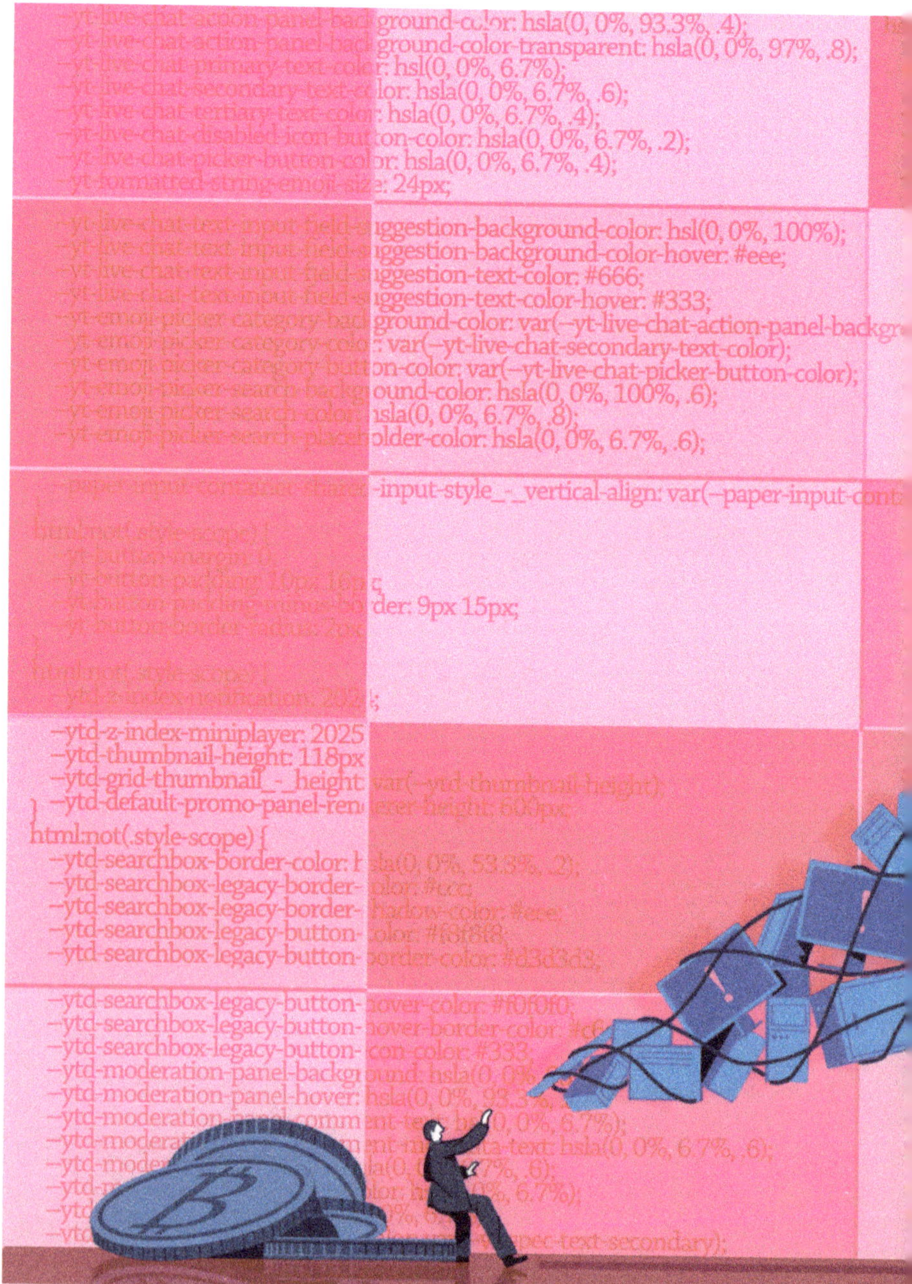
--yt-live-chat-action-panel-background-color-transparent: hsla(0, 0%, 97%, .8);
--yt-live-chat-primary-text-color: hsl(0, 0%, 6.7%);
--yt-live-chat-secondary-text-color: hsla(0, 0%, 6.7%, .6);
--yt-live-chat-tertiary-text-color: hsla(0, 0%, 6.7%, .4);
--yt-live-chat-disabled-icon-button-color: hsla(0, 0%, 6.7%, .2);
--yt-live-chat-picker-button-color: hsla(0, 0%, 6.7%, .4);
--yt-formatted-string-emoji-size: 24px;
--yt-live-chat-text-input-field-suggestion-background-color: hsl(0, 0%, 100%);
--yt-live-chat-text-input-field-suggestion-background-color-hover: #eee;
--yt-live-chat-text-input-field-suggestion-text-color: #666;
--yt-live-chat-text-input-field-suggestion-text-color-hover: #333;
--yt-emoji-picker-category-color: var(--yt-live-chat-secondary-text-color);
--yt-emoji-picker-category-button-color: var(--yt-live-chat-picker-button-color);
--yt-emoji-picker-search-background-color: hsla(0, 0%, 100%, .6);
--yt-emoji-picker-search-color: hsla(0, 0%, 6.7%, .8);
--yt-emoji-picker-search-placeholder-color: hsla(0, 0%, 6.7%, .6);
--ytd-z-index-miniplayer: 2025
--ytd-thumbnail-height: 118px
--ytd-grid-thumbnail_-_height: var(--ytd-thumbnail-height);
--ytd-default-promo-panel-renderer-height: 600px;
html:not(.style-scope) {
--ytd-searchbox-border-color: hsla(0, 0%, 53.3%, .2);
--ytd-searchbox-legacy-border-color: #ccc;
--ytd-searchbox-legacy-border-shadow-color: #eee;
--ytd-searchbox-legacy-button-color: #f8f8f8;
--ytd-searchbox-legacy-button-border-color: #d3d3d3;
--ytd-searchbox-legacy-button-hover-color: #f0f0f0;
--ytd-searchbox-legacy-button-icon-color: #333;
--ytd-moderation-panel-hover: hsla(0, 0%, 93.3%,

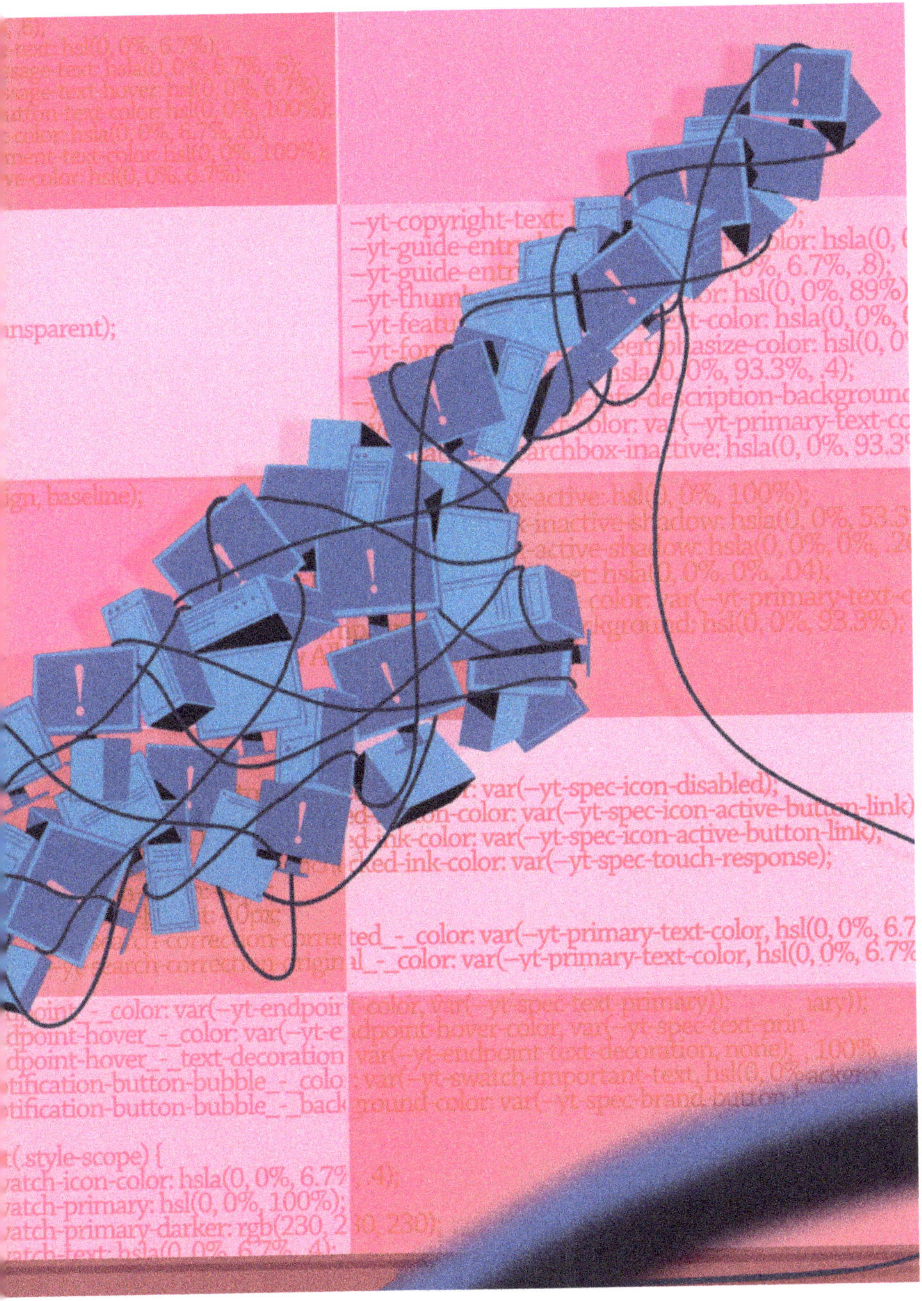

nsparent);
—yt-copyright-text:
—yt-guide-entr
—yt-guide-entr
—yt-thumb
—yt-featu
—yt-fon
olor: hsla(0,
0%, 6.7%, .8);
olor: hsl(0, 0%, 89%)
t-color: hsla(0, 0%,
asize-color: hsl(0, 0
hsla(0, 0%, 93.3%, .4);
description-background
color: var(—yt-primary-text-co
archbox-inactive: hsla(0, 0%, 93.3
gn, baseline);
x-active: hsl(0, 0%, 100%);
-inactive-shadow: hsla(0, 0%, 53.3
-active-shadow: hsla(0, 0%, 0%, .2
t: hsla(0, 0%, 0%, .04);
color: var(—yt-primary-text-c
kground: hsl(0, 0%, 93.3%);
: var(—yt-spec-icon-disabled);
icon-color: var(—yt-spec-icon-active-button-link)
ed-ink-color: var(—yt-spec-icon-active-button-link);
ked-ink-color: var(—yt-spec-touch-response);
ted_-_color: var(—yt-primary-text-color, hsl(0, 0%, 6.7
l_-_color: var(—yt-primary-text-color, hsl(0, 0%, 6.7%
dpoint-hover_-_color: var(—yt-e
dpoint-hover_-_text-decoration
tification-button-bubble_-_colo
tification-button-bubble_-_back
(.style-scope) {
vatch-icon-color: hsla(0, 0%, 6.7%, .4);
vatch-primary: hsl(0, 0%, 100%);
vatch-primary-darker: rgb(230, 230, 230);

66 Fork

We all know that blockchain is an open and transparent open-source project. A set of codes in the client software specifies the rules of trading and mining. Open source means that everyone can see all the details of the construction of this "palace" that subverts all cognition and has the opportunity to rewrite the open code per their beliefs.

Therefore, the client supporting the blockchain's operation is dynamically updated in real time. Under the condition that the client is updated, each release of a software protocol's new version is called a fork.

Forks occur the most frequently in Bitcoin. The protocol of the Bitcoin client has been updated many times, although most of the forks have been unknown. Some are meant to patch security loopholes, while others are designed to add new features to smooth transactions.

A situation like this may have happened to you in real life: One day, you found a tiny red dot on an app when you turned on your mobile phone. You found it not working after launching it unless you could download the app's updated version.

You may have been used to following software instructions faithfully. But have you ever thought of a centralized organization behind all this? It has the right to stop you from continuing to use the original version. That is equivalent to covertly taking away your right to use it and forcing you to download a new version.

So, let's go back to the decentralized operation of Bitcoin and think about what would happen every time a client forked once without a "center" to force every participant to use the new version.

It's normal for people to put off or give up updating a version since everyone can autonomously decide whether to accept a new protocol. As a result, the client version in each user's hands may be inconsistent. What's worse, it can never be in uniform.

Those participants who have upgraded their client software publish transactions that conform to the new protocol. In contrast, those who continue using the old software version post their transactions conforming to the old protocol. Consequently, transactions generated under both old and new protocols likely exist in the network at the same time.

Things become a bit complicated because these different participants have to publish their transactions and use the client to verify other people's transactions. In this ecosystem where old and new protocols coexist, the criteria for determining whether a transaction is legal are likely to pole apart.

On the other hand, despite the difference in versions, protocols, and mutually agreed-upon rules, these participants operate on the same blockchain. Therefore, they must work out a solution.

In fact, because it is an entirely autonomous ecology, participants will naturally generate a new steady state out of consideration of self-interest in such a complex situation.

It's like in different conventional cultures on the same planet, where the same behavior may represent completely different emotions. The same thumbs-up gesture is a symbol of compliment in China, a curse in Australia, and an insult in Nigeria, and you must be careful in the last case. You can imagine if three people of the varying cultural backgrounds got together, they would either have to be tolerant and get along in harmony or squabble with each other and part in displeasure.

That is the prototype of the two scenarios happening to different participants after the fork has emerged.

67 Soft Fork

All blockchain client users initially run the same version of the software, following the same set of rules and protocols that stipulate the block size and transformation format. After the fork, clients of various versions began to coexist, and the phenomenon of transactions conforming to both the old and new protocols appeared simultaneously on a blockchain.

Under this circumstance, an old protocol may determine that a transaction generated per the new protocol is also legitimate. This fork can be called a soft fork. In other words, the soft fork eventually caused the old and new protocols to become compatible.

But if you better understand how the fork has achieved consensus through self-governance, you'll find that it hasn't done so overnight. It has been a process of fierce contest among different interest groups.

Now, let's look at how the whole process works.

You must understand that most soft forks are about adding new functionality to a transaction. For example, to alleviate the congestion of the Bitcoin network, some developers thought of increasing the capacity of the block and added a critical function called Segwit so that the blocks generated under the new protocol can accommodate the equivalent of the original two to three times the number of transactions.

Interestingly, the developers who initiated this fork used some small tricks when writing the code so that the old protocol could fully adopt the new protocol. In theory, when the block capacity generated under the new protocol is significantly increased and exceeds the original 1MB size limit, the old protocol will refuse to pass the verification because the block is illegal. It's equivalent to the situation where your luggage is found overweight at the airport check-in window, and if you don't want to comply with the airline's rules, you won't be allowed to pass the checkpoint.

But the developer's "trick" is to unknowingly let participants who haven't updated the client version complete the verification of the blocks generated under the new protocol. Some trick was played while writing the new protocol to isolate a part of the data in the transaction so that the old protocol cannot recognize this part of the data when calculating the block capacity. Therefore, the capacity still won't exceed 1MB.

It sounds tricky, doesn't it?

In fact, Satoshi Nakamoto used a similar trick to change the Bitcoin block size from 32MB to 1MB in the early years. In the earliest soft fork, the old protocol also passed a verification because it failed to recognize the new protocol's modifications.

But the old protocol may be compatible with the new protocol. However, since the new protocol treats some or all of the blocks generated under the old one as illegal, those participants who have updated the client version will ruthlessly show the red light. Consequently, such a phenomenon has emerged in the ecology: The blocks generated under the new protocol will be accepted by the users of the old protocol. In contrast, the new protocol users will exclude the blocks generated under the old protocol.

In this case, miners supporting the old and new protocols are isolated from each other, and the entire blockchain faces the risk of split. They worry that it will affect the whole ecosystem in the long run, causing the currency's price to drop. Eventually, miners supporting the old protocol chose to upgrade their clients. The entire blockchain remains the same after a temporary version divergence. This process is called an instance of a soft fork.

You can compare this soft fork to Microsoft Office's accommodation of the old and new versions. A file created with the 2016 version can be successfully opened with the 2011 version. It's equivalent to the transactions generated under the new protocol in a blockchain being accepted by the old protocol. However, some new features of the 2016 version of Microsoft Office don't work in the 2011 version.

If some new features have become necessary for office work, users with the old version will eventually switch to the latest version due to financial interests.

68 Hard Fork

Some public blockchains like Bitcoin and Ethereum initially caught the attention of only a small group of fanatics. They have eventually evolved into something embraced by an increasingly growing number of people who swarm into this ecosystem. Different values and interest demands have emerged in the blockchain community. In essence, the fork is a process of interest redistribution.

SegWit, mentioned in the previous example of Bitcoin's soft fork, can be regarded as "a round-about way" of making changes through slight code modification, increasing the block size from 1MB several times. However, others have chosen to fall out with the rest to increase the blocks' size.

Some angry "rebels" insist on raising the ceiling of Bitcoin block size. However, they are either unwilling (or unable) to use small technical tricks to achieve an internal agreement between the old and the new protocols. So they took it upon themselves to develop an independent protocol that was neither compatible nor acceptable by the old protocol, resulting in forming opposition camps between supporters and opponents of block expansion.

The old protocol doesn't recognize the legitimacy of the blocks generated under the new protocol. Compared with the quiet "revolution" of the soft fork, the "uprising" of this hard fork is like pouring oil on the fire.

However, the new protocol doesn't find itself at a dead end because its supporters strive to maintain the same chain instead of building their separate ones.

Bitcoin Cash is a classic case of "flying solo" due to the breakup concerning the consensus about block size expansion. Eager to leave the Bitcoin ecosystem forever, those participants looking for large-capacity blocks built a new blockchain according to their beliefs, with its core code drawing on Bitcoin.

Since then, there has been a hard fork within Bitcoin Cash due to a disagreement with the concept. Since the public blockchain is decentralized, every participant has the right to initiate a fork.

You may wonder if the blockchain ecosystem is stable.

Remember, the laws of human nature won't fail in any ecology, whether decentralized or not. Those conflicts of interest originating from human nature have never changed. But the beauty of the blockchain community is that each participant can contribute their computing power to express support or opposition to a particular decision.

Suppose you have developed a protocol to create a new chain. However, no one or very few people support your protocol, and people remain in the original protocol framework to continue mining. In theory, you can mine in your new chain, but because the value of the mined coins has not been widely recognized, your work has become a self-entertainment. Therefore, such a hard fork only makes sense if the new chain can also obtain sufficient computing power support.

Of course, there have also been stories with a happy ending in the history of Bitcoin's hard fork. For example, the Bitcoin developing team discovered a flaw that could change the original constant circulation into unlimited quantity. They then patched this vulnerability in a new version. Although it was a hard fork that required everyone to upgrade the client version simultaneously, it didn't result in any splits because everyone involved agreed with the new protocol.

As interests become increasingly intertwined, there have indeed been hard forks initiated purely for self-gains, throwing the blockchain community into turbulence. However, blockchain is a decentralized ecosystem where people vote with their feet. Cinderella-like miracles may happen for a time. But like some junk stocks hyped by capital, the blockchains formed by hard forks without core values eventually sink into public oblivion.

69 SegWit

We mentioned "SegWit" when we explained the soft folk. It's short for Segregated Witness, a scheme used primarily to expand the Bitcoin block capacity.

The problem of Bitcoin network congestion has always been the focus of all intelligent people.

In this era of "instant" gratification, wherever you find yourself, you may not think that the seemingly all-powerful Bitcoin transaction still has a time-lapse. You must have been used to the convenience of thumbing your WeChat, Alipay, or some mobile phone bank software, with which you can instantly transfer money to the other party's account. But you must wait when you come to the Bitcoin network.

The reason is simple: Your bookkeeper isn't a centralized institution. Miners need to decide the outcome of mining through free competition and choose the time to serve their customers based on the level of miner fees they can pay. As more and more people use Bitcoin, they find the original 1MB block too small a capacity to accommodate more transactions, making the entire network inefficient, especially for ordinary traders who don't want to pay more.

So the developers thought of SegWit.

Let's first look at what the "witness" means in Segregated Witness.

A Bitcoin block contains several transactions, which fall into two parts. One you can easily imagine is the transfer-out, transfer-in address, and transfer amount. It's very similar to the information on the bank statement, isn't it?

You can hardly find a real-life counterpart of the second part. Miners use this part of the information to verify that the transfer initiator truly has the right to use the funds. It's called the "witness" information.

Let's return to SegWit. As the name suggests, it isolates the "witness" information so that it is not counted into the block capacity.

A lot of block space can be freed up this way because the "witness" information often takes up a large volume of space in a transaction. With SegWit enabled, the "witness" information is excluded from the block size calculation. As a result, a block that can only hold 1MB of data initially can be filled with 2 to 3MB of data.

It's like taking a bus that can accommodate a limited number of people. SegWit is equivalent to throwing everyone's luggage and luggage on the roof so more passengers can be squeezed into the limited space. In addition to solving the block size problem, another function of SegWit is to fix a bug in the old protocol initially used by Bitcoin.

With some understanding of this bug, you can find how hard geeks have worked to create a near-perfect Bitcoin ecosystem.

As we mentioned before, when you initiate a transaction, you must add a digital signature with the private key to prove to the miners that you're the actual owner of a specific bitcoin. The signature transmission means, "I am the owner of this bitcoin."

After you publish the transaction, you'll get a transaction ID composed of numbers and letters generated through hashing your transaction information. It's like the receipt you receive during a fund transfer in a bank. If the recipient lied that he didn't receive the bitcoin in the future, you could show the ID to prove it.

But there is a small time window here. After the Bitcoin transaction is published, it needs to wait for a period on the network before miners package it into the block. What if a malicious person secretly changes your digital signature during this period?

Imagine what will happen next. The easiest thing you can think of is that miners cannot pass the verification, right? Indeed, a miner can't verify a tampered signature, but nothing is certain.

This eccentric villain may not have tampered with your digital signature completely but secretly changed the "format" for you on a whim, turning the statement "I am the owner of this bitcoin" into "This bitcoin is mine." Since both formats express the same meaning, miners can still pass the verification without suspicion. It's equivalent to introducing your brother. You can say, "He's my brother" or "I'm his sister," without affecting the meaning.

But here arises a problem. The transaction ID in your hand is derived from hashing the transaction information when you send the transfer request. Given the characteristics of the hash algorithm, although the meaning hasn't changed, the transaction ID has altered after the villain modifies the "format."

The ID that the miner sees is the modified hash, and it's this hash that is concatenated into the block.

Good Heavens! The transaction ID on the chain differs from the one in your hand. If you have to confront the recipient in the future, you won't have direct evidence to protect your interest.

It sounds like a bug, but it's infrequent in the Bitcoin network. After all, this kind of malpractice won't affect the conclusion of the transaction, and the evildoer won't benefit from it. Still, perfectionist geeks feel thrilled to be able to fix this bug.

With SegWit, the digital signature is also classified as "witness" information, as the one used by miners for verification. When a transaction ID is generated, it won't be calculated and hashed together. This way, the transaction ID won't be changed, no matter how the perpetrator modifies the digital signature format.

I'm using so much real property of this book for dwelling upon this bug to show the Bitcoin believers' best effort to improve this decentralized ecology in a seemingly obsessive-compulsive manner. Perhaps, the fascinating beauty of coding is its total metaphysical triumph.

Finally, it's worth mentioning that the Bitcoin Core's development team proposed SegWit in 2015 to file Bitcoin's expansion on record. Since then, the plan's implementation has gone through ups and downs due to objections from other interest groups. However, it eventually gained 95% of the computing power and was successfully activated on August 24, 2017, Beijing Time.

70 SegWit2x

When introducing SegWit, we were unconsciously moved by the fighting spirit of the geeks. However, the code may be innocent, but the people who write it aren't necessarily.

The protracted war between mining farms, mining pools, and the Bitcoin Core's development team has outlined the rift in the various interests of the massive Bitcoin network, and the powder keg is SegWit2x.

We might as well take a close look at its struggling history. The names might show that SegWit2x is SegWit 2.0., but the former had appeared before the latter was activated. However, in terms of its core values, it also advocates the isolation of "witness" information to expand the block capacity in disguise.

The Bitcoin Core's development team proposed this solution. They primarily developed and updated the Bitcoin client after Satoshi Nakamoto's retirement. But it was challenging to get the support of mining farms and pools that concentrated a lot of computing power by using this solution to expand the block capacity.

Mining farms and pools are more concerned about bitcoin prices and transaction fees because they have invested a lot of mining equipment to seek benefits from mining.

The development team proposed SegWit to pave the way for the future deployment of the Lightning Network, which advocates that many small

transactions should not be placed on the blockchain but be processed "off the chain" in another form. It reduces the miners' income and violates the interests of the mining farms and pools.

On the other hand, the Lightning Network is developed by a third-party centralized organization, and several people controlling the organization are key members of the Bitcoin Core's development team. Mining farms and pools feel their position in the Bitcoin ecosystem has been shaken.

Therefore, owners of the farms and pools favor a plan to expand the block directly rather than adding SegWit functions.

But the Bitcoin Core's development team objects that once the plan goes ahead, it can no longer reject the subsequent proposal to increase the blocks, which will, in turn, increase the volume of the blockchain's ledger. Once the storage capacity of personal computers maxes, transaction information has to be stored in mining farms and pools, resulting in Bitcoin's centralization.

After disagreeing and bickering for years, the two sides finally decided to compromise. In 2015, they allowed miners to upgrade to a new version of the Bitcoin client with the SegWit function activated. That was the soft fork initiated by the Bitcoin Core's development team. The team promised to continue expanding the blockchain in the future as a condition for the compromise.

However, the two sides seemed to have reached a consensus, but their contention intensified instead of being eased.

Owners of mining farms and pools, exchanges, and wallet providers met in New York City and signed a new protocol, which is SegWit2x, under discussion. The primary initiative of SegWit2x is that three months after the activation of SegWit in August, the Bitcoin Core's development team must support the blocks' expansion.

Though dubbed "New York Consensus," it looks more like a unilateral initiative because, on the long list of signers representing 83% of the computing power of the entire Bitcoin network, only the signature of the Bitcoin Core's development team is absent.

It set the tone for the ill fate of SegWit2x subsequently. Having lost trust in the Bitcoin Core's development team, the mining farms and pools decided to develop a new Bitcoin Cash chain independent of the Bitcoin ecosystem through a "violent" hard fork before SegWit was fully activated. They also increased the block size of Bitcoin Cash from the original 1MB to 8MB per their own conception while refusing to add the SegWit function.

SegWit, launched about a year, was finally successfully activated in August 2017. But SegWit2x's advocacy for expanding the block in three months was aborted.

Some "big block" supporters directly invested their computing power in Bitcoin Cash generated by the fork. The SegWit2x agreement, signed in haste, failed to build broad community support regarding some fundamental technological issues. The list of proponents on the "New York Consensus" was shortened gradually. The supporting computing power dropped 66% from 83% in about a dozen days.

The story ended with the SegWit program's announcement of its termination in November 2017.

SegWit2x's "abortion" is a problem that every follower of the belief in decentralization must face. The struggle for ecological rights may not seem noble enough, but it's life. Humans are also strongly driven by self-interest, even in a world of "decentralization" that shimmers with idealism and utopian blips. This contention among various interest groups becomes more complex without the constraint of a single centralized value. All you see is the result of balancing and rebalancing interests.

- **Related vocabulary**

  Lightning Network

71 Lightning Network

Bitcoin is a living ecosystem that can purify and adjust itself from time to time. SegWit's solution allows more transaction data to be inserted into each block to increase the efficiency of the entire network in processing transactions. It's like having more people sharing a table in a restaurant to cut other customers' waiting time. The fans of "big blocks" flew solo and established a new blockchain.

The Lightning Network is also a solution to the efficiency problem. The idea is similar to opening a carry-out window to divert impatient customers from a restaurant with limited seating.

Suppose you and your partner want to transfer bitcoins quickly now. You need to download a kind of wallet software with Lightning Network function. Once you enable this function, you seem to open up a fast transfer channel only for the two of you.

This channel is a shared "account" similar to a fund pool. You must deposit some bitcoins into the account before completing transfers of your funds on this channel.

The miners will only package and insert into the block the amount you deposited when opening the channel and the distribution information of the account balance when you close it. They don't have to record each of your transactions on a blockchain. Therefore, you don't have to wait in line to have your funds transferred to your account in real time when conducting the transactions.

However, since your transactions on the Lightning Network are not on the chain, are they prone to fraud? In fact, there are also some protection mechanisms intrinsic to the Lightning Network. If you're trading on it as an advocate of closing the channel, you must wait about a week to get the balance transferred into your account.

In addition, the Lightning Network also has a set of punishment mechanisms to deter those potential defrauders with severe punishment.

Ethereum also has a similar block expansion plan known as the "Thunder Network." From its name, it follows that it must be Lightning Network's "close relative."

The Lightning Network essentially offloads some transactions from the chain.

Imagine this scenario: No matter how many transactions you and your partners have privately conducted on the fast channel, only the information produced at the channel's closure needs to be packaged and connected to the chain. Does this practice affect the miners' interests? Each transaction generates a miner fee to reward the miners for bookkeeping. However, while improving the transaction efficiency, the Lightning Network inflicts losses on the miners. Therefore, the network's activation has witnessed wranglings among conflicting interests.

The shadow of Bitcoin's capacity has always been hanging over the ecosystem. Satoshi Nakamoto had initially set the size of a single block to

32MB. But he eventually reduced it to 1MB for fear that the stored ledger would have become so large that a blockchain could have been a game of influential financial magnates. His consideration maintains the dignity of decentralization design to the greatest extent but has inadvertently created a chain reaction. We believe that struggles and disputes will continue before the problem is solved. We must admit that each progress toward the ideal of decentralization will be hard-earned.

72 State Channel

When we introduced SegWit, we said that this technology is designed to isolate "witness information" and keep it outside the block to expand the number of transactions stored in a Bitcoin block. The state channel records the "state information" on a unique "channel" without taking up the block's space. The state channel, like SegWit, is also a solution for block expansion.

What is "state information," then?

You'll see your balance amount in the wallet when you launch your WeChat. The number tells you the state of your account. The state is refreshed whenever you transfer some funds or receive a red cash envelope. It's a piece of state information.

You can now treat Bitcoin as a payment app as well. Each of your transactions will be recorded by a blockchain, and each record will refresh your personal state information. Since the blockchain's state information is

composed of all the people on the blockchain, one person's transaction will change everyone else's "state" on the blockchain network accordingly.

Proponents of the state channel technology believe that Bitcoin's congestion is due to such a process: Each time you conduct a transaction, which is translated into updating your balance, miners must verify and record it on the chain.

With the state channel technology, both parties can open up another "channel" for the transaction. No matter how frequently they trade on this "channel" and how many times the state changes, the balance information of both parties will eventually be inserted into the Bitcoin block only when the channel is closed.

You must have also discovered that the Lightning Network is an application of state channel technology.

For some blockchain application projects that require frequent responses, state channel technology can also optimize the experience. Suppose there's an underlying Go app using blockchain technology, and each of the moves played by you and your opponent is recorded on the chain. In that case, every information is broadcast to the network to wait for miners' verification and confirmation, and you must pay miner fees.

The advantage of the state channel presents itself because only the winning and losing states of the game when it is begun and finished are recorded on the blockchain. In the meantime, no matter how you move your pieces, you only update the state on the "channel" established by you and your opponent. It not only makes the system respond faster but also prevents you from paying extra miner fees.

73 Bitcoin Core's Development Team

In 2009, Satoshi Nakamoto, the Father of Bitcoin, released the first version of the Bitcoin client, Bitcoin Core. From the beginning, he wrote Bitcoin's transaction, consensus, total volume, and other settings into the client.

The client allows you to connect to the Bitcoin network, create your address, conduct bitcoin transactions, and check your bitcoin balance. You perform all the operations through a code, the Bitcoin protocol.

Like a newborn, the fledgling Bitcoin protocol needs constant improvement and maintenance, such as fixing its security bugs or changing the agreement.

However, the most mysterious eccentric in the digital world quietly retired after posting his last message on the Internet in 2010, handing over the responsibility of maintaining the Bitcoin protocol to other program developers who participated in the early development.

Since Bitcoin is an open-source project, theoretically, anyone can participate in its maintenance. As Bitcoin is getting more influential, the number of participating programmers has significantly increased, thus forming the Bitcoin Core's development team.

Interestingly, the team doesn't have a leader. Neither does it determine who is eligible to join. It even doesn't have a date for its establishment. The team members are all programmers who voluntarily contribute to the Bitcoin protocol. They can come and go of their free will.

Developers who have made outstanding contributions at one time may disappear in the blink of an eye. This group of people is putting the decentralized ideal of Bitcoin into practice.

The nature of decentralization dictates their behavior. When the Bitcoin protocol called for changes, the team had no authority to get a unified statement from its members. Therefore, it was not at all surprising for disagreement to arise among the members, who chose to leave and establish

new Bitcoin clients that conform to their ideals.

The most famous event here, also the best-known event of the Bitcoin Core's development team, is the battle for the Bitcoin block expansion scheme introduced earlier.

Bitcoin's block size is only 1MB, which cannot meet the growing transaction demands. The developers claiming to uphold Satoshi Nakamoto's original intention are behind the efforts to maintain the block's initial size and advocate placing small transactions off-chain to relieve the pressure from the blockchain. But, among the big-block supporters keen on the hard fork after their relationship with the other party soured were active early members of the Bitcoin Core's development team.

The value of decentralization gave each of Bitcoin Core's development team members the greatest freedom, like an erratic club. They came together because of their shared belief in an alternative world. They also broke up due to divergent interests: It could arise from the self-evaluation of their internal growth or disputes between members. Various challenges and risks may accompany decentralization, but its inherent logic deserves the applause of this era.

74 Zero-confirmation Transaction

Zero-confirmation transactions have been broadcast to the blockchain network but have not yet been stuffed into blocks by miners. Let's take a look at what "confirmation" means.

About every 10 minutes, a batch of transactions in the Bitcoin network is stuffed into a block "hot from the grill." This new block is added to the very end of the blockchain. After miners' verification, a transaction inserted into a block is said to have received a "confirmation." It gets a second "confirmation" if a new block is added after it. And the process goes on and on.

Your transaction must be "confirmed" and added to the blockchain before completion.

When I introduced the concept of "double payment," I mentioned that some perpetrators would spend a sum of Bitcoin before this record is connected to the blockchain by miners. They then take the opportunity of the fleeting interval to initiate a second transaction with the same bitcoin. Although the two transactions will eventually fail to pass the miners' verification, they still succeed in their evildoing if the sellers have already shipped the goods without waiting for "confirmation."

Generally speaking, more "confirmations" will keep your transactions safer, but at the cost of your waiting time.

However, Bitcoin Cash, isolated from the Bitcoin ecosystem by the hard fork, consists of many participants supporting zero-confirmation transactions. Many merchants in the Bitcoin Cash community also embrace such a service.

If you pay a sum of Bitcoin Cash, the merchant's wallet app will display a notification like this: "A sum of Bitcoin Cash is coming to you." It is a

reminder that a transaction has been broadcast, but miners haven't yet verified it.

It is equivalent to a business partner initiating an interbank transfer of funds to you through a bank app, which sends you a screenshot of the transfer slip. It might give you enough peace of mind, although it will take 1-2 business days for the money to be transferred to the account under your name.

By accepting zero-confirmation transactions, the time of the transaction between the merchant and you is considerably shortened because the whole process omits the waiting for miners to verify and package data on the chain.

The rationale behind Bitcoin Cash's support for zero-confirmation transactions is that double-spending occurs with an extremely low probability. However, the issue isn't that simple.

Regardless of the probability of damage to the remittees' interests, the firepower of criticism against this logic has focused on other aspects. Let's go back to the assumption that you are a consumer about to spend Bitcoin Cash. Let's look at what would happen once you initiate a transaction that triggers a double-spending on a blockchain with zero confirmation transactions added.

While a new block hasn't been mined, a miner selected your transaction. After a while, he sees another transaction conflicting with the verification information of your transaction. In this situation, he will pick and mark the transaction he approves. Other miners will recognize his verification when seeing the identifier. The other transaction will consequently be abandoned.

By now, the new block has been mined. The identified transaction is logically inserted into the new block.

Did you find the problem arising? When judging which transaction is legitimate, miners may not follow objective criteria. Instead, they make their decisions themselves. In practice, such an operation gives too much power to miners.

Few miners today are working solo. They would instead contribute their computing power to mining pools to mine in groups. If a mining pool has too much final say while a currency accepts zero-confirmation transactions, it may run the risk of becoming centralized against the original rules of decentralization.

75 Homomorphic Hashing

We have detailed the rules of hashing. Hashing is reliable because as long as the plaintext is slightly modified, the hash value will be completely unrecognizable, so it can be used to check whether a plaintext has been doctored.

Suppose you divide the 300,000-word *One Hundred Years of Solitude* into two parts and hash their contents separately. In that case, you'll get two hash values. But the result you get from combining the two hashes will be meaningless because the outcome has nothing to do with either. That's the regular hash.

Homomorphic hashing is a special kind of hashing. After homomorphic hashing, the sum of the upper and lower values is equivalent to the result

obtained by hashing the entire *One Hundred Years of Solitude* book at once.

Using homomorphic hashing can reduce the amount of computation. Let's assume you store a piece of data, calculate its hash value, and save it. In a few days, you need to update the data. After submitting the updated data, you only need to hash the updated part and add it to the original hash value without having to hash the entire data again.

Some miracles will happen when homomorphic hashing and blockchain are put together. For example, suppose you want to try DNA sequencing to test whether you risk developing a disease. DNA sequencing companies in the real world may draw conclusions by crunching the data. But it will get hold of all your private information simultaneously.

What will happen if data calculation is done by the smart contract that uses the homomorphic hashing technology?

Your private data remains invisible to the gene sequencing company and the entire blockchain because it's been hashed. But homomorphically hashed data can still be calculated. Did you see that the DNA company can still do sequencing without seeing the private data in this scenario?

The homomorphic hashing's function of "concealment" is quite in line with the blockchain's pursuit because it can improve the privacy of transactions. If it's used for cryptocurrency transactions, miners can complete the verification of some transaction information without seeing both parties' addresses and amounts.

76 Zero Knowledge Proof

One person wants to prove an argument against another person, and he uses a method of proof that ensures that the other person can't obtain additional information beyond what is already known. This method of proof is called zero-knowledge proof.

In the context of blockchain, a transaction initiator can prove to the miners that his transaction is legal without telling them additional information, such as the addresses of both trading parties and the transaction amount. Such an operation uses the principles of zero knowledge proof.

It sounds a bit abstract, doesn't it? You may as well join me in a specific scenario. A guy who claims to be the gatekeeper of the Museum of Modern Art in New York City and touts the key to the museum, saying that he can prove his identity in two ways:

First, he opens the door to the museum and takes you in to prove the key's authenticity. But by doing so, the collection of masterpieces is exposed.

Second, everyone knows the museum's prized treasure is the original work of Van Gogh's *Starry Night*. The gatekeeper can get only the painting out and show it to you. This way, he can prove he has the genuine key without exposing the other masterpieces in the museum's collection.

The second way to prove that you have a genuine key is zero knowledge proof. Like everyone else, you won't know any museum holdings other than *Starry Night* while proving the key.

We can use another example to explain the concept. Here are two balls of the same size. Alice tells color-blinded Bob that the two balls are of different colors. Bob wants Alice to prove it. So, he holds a ball in each hand and asks Alice to turn her back to him. Bob can decide if he would switch the balls and ask Alice to turn around and tell him if he has done so.

If Alice gives him the correct answer, two possibilities may occur: The balls' colors vary, or their color is the same, only that Alice has made a lucky guess. Then, Bob repeats the Question & Answer game 100 times and requests that Alice's answers be correct in every instance to prove what she says is the truth. Bob does this because he believes the probability of 100 consecutive pairings is almost zero.

After the proving game, Bob still knows that the two balls' colors are different without knowing what colors they are.

What does zero-knowledge proof bring to blockchain?

Transactions in a blockchain are visible to everyone in the network. Zero knowledge proof allows an asset to be transferred with privacy in mind. Not only does the miner verifying the transaction have no way of knowing the transaction information, but except for the information that a verified transaction has occurred, others in the network know nothing about the transaction participants' identities and the transaction amount.

77 Interchangeability

As a member of Gen Z, you're used to going out without cash. But, one day, a retailer's electronic payment system failed, so you had to borrow a 20 yuan bill from a friend. The next day, you returned him another banknote of the same denomination. He accepted happily because the two notes had the same value. That means they are interchangeable though they are different banknotes with other serial numbers. That is currency interchangeability.

Interchangeability is the essential property of currency. If this property weren't ensured, the currency system would collapse.

Unfortunately, Bitcoin may still have an "interchangeability crisis" even when a few countries have recognized it as a currency.

Perhaps, you didn't expect that the bitcoins you have may be rejected under some particular circumstances.

Where the conventional banknotes and coins are concerned, no one knows whose hands they have passed before coming to you. Therefore, the history of their transactions is untraceable. In other words, the information behind every banknote or coin in circulation can be considered the same, which is a vital pivot of interchangeability.

However, Bitcoin is a transparent and open electronic currency system. Other people may not match those who transfer and receive cryptocurrencies with their real-world identities and transactions. However, each bitcoin transfer from one address to another can always be traced and

never be doctored. They are recorded on a blockchain as undeniable proof. Therefore, if someone is careful enough, he can always figure out the parties to a transaction. For example, if someone has bought and sold bitcoins at an exchange, where he must submit his identity information, his real identity may be exposed.

You can understand it this way: Although a new world seems to have been established beyond the real world's rules of the game, some people in the real world have genuine clues about some coin possessors and "blacklist" their addresses with every reason.

It's easy to understand. Suppose your bitcoins are found to be associated with an address considered to have an unpopular transaction background. In that case, your coins may be rejected. In other words, they've lost their "interchangeability" within a certain measure of value.

Those uninterchangeable bitcoins would be worthless, maintaining only the price at face value. Newly "mined" bitcoins are the most popular, and only they are pure because they have no visible transaction history.

In retrospect, we can now realize why so many new technologies strive for cryptocurrency's anonymity. The technologies I've introduced, such as the ring signature, homomorphic hashing, and zero knowledge confirmation, are all designed to free themselves from the fear of the "interchangeability crisis."

PART

5

Past Events and Present Tense

78 ICO

Many people know what IPO is. It's short for "Initial Public Offering," which means that a company publicly sells its stock to the public. ICO is the abbreviation of "Initial Crypto-Token Offering," which means that a blockchain company publicly sells its Token to the public for the first time. There is clearly a connection between the two.

It's generally suggested that ICOs be seen as IPOs in cryptocurrency. At least, those ICO designers have preached so to the public.

Here's how ICO financing works: The party with a project must first publish a document known as a "white paper" to introduce the project's business model, technical features, timeline, and capital allocation. Of course, it doesn't matter if someone wants to insert an excerpt from *Harry Potter* into the document on a whim. After all, there's no central agency like the Stock Issuance Examination and Verification Committee to determine if the "white paper" is eligible to be released to the public.

Suppose you are an investor who wants to participate in an ICO. Once the "white paper's" narrative impresses you, you can express support for launching the project with the cryptocurrencies in your wallet, usually bitcoins or ethers. A start-up company is like a sprouting seed; it must go through trials and tribulations before it can be eligible for an IPO. But it requires only a company's faint "fetal movement" story to issue an ICO.

You may wonder if it's a bit like crowdfunding. It's true, except that only bitcoins or ethers rather than actual currency can be raised with ICOs to eliminate the risk of being accused of financial fundraising fraud by investors. In reality, the project party can exchange these cryptocurrencies for real ones at any time, following the constraints of the "white paper."

You pay bitcoins or ethers to get the reward of the Token the project has issued. It's equivalent to your "holding" certificate.

What prompts you to make a decision at this moment may be a vivid, unrestrained imagination: Tokens will be circulated in the future project ecology and used to purchase products and services. You can also sell the value-added Token for profit as the project grows. But the harsh reality is that your interests are entirely based on the ethical foundation of the project party's trustworthiness and the business environment as you wish. At the same time, your bitcoins or ethers have already been transferred to their address in advance.

Followers of ICOs believe that by accumulating the power of seed users who hold Token and pooling small and micro funds, they can help the project party verify the feasibility of innovation between "vision" and "action." But real human nature is more like a magic mirror in the hands of a dark force. Instead of illuminating the boundaries of decentralization, it has turned the carnival into perverse and barbaric speculation.

When you open an app on a stock exchange, you'll see one company after another that the Securities Regulatory Commission has approved behind the thousands of red or green numbers. The criteria for approval include multi-dimensions such as performance and compliance. But in a pure blockchain world, there is no so-called "approval," and no institution can exercise such supreme power. Therefore, the evaluation of ICO projects lacks an external basis.

Returning to the project proper, you'll find the various footprints of a company's development in the prospectus. In the dossier of an ICO initiator's profile, you can only find sugar-coated tall tales.

The ICO miracle is nothing but a bloody history of capital. From the beginning of 2014 to the end of 2018, the amount of financing through ICOs exceeded 20 billion US Dollars. However, over half of the projects declared bankruptcy within four months of launching their ICOs. Several critics have pointed out that 99.9% of ICOs are scams or rubbish.

As an investor, you can only drift along blindfolded with your Tokens that may be worthless tomorrow.

On September 4, 2017, the Chinese government finally issued an across-the-board ban on ICOs. It popped many a mesmerizing bubble of money and desire like a sharp needle. ICO has since remained a derogatory term.

ICOs may have been a benign idea at first. However, it's more like a fig leaf over the greedy nature of humanity today when the public is generally uneducated and therefore irrational about the blockchain and Token.

A fundamental question will be asked even in the future: Is it necessary to set a threshold for launching ICOs, and should ICOs be centrally regulated like IPOs? If you think carefully, you'll discover no perfect answer.

79 White Paper

You may come across a "white paper" in your daily life, which is often an authoritative report or guide that briefly explains a complex issue and focuses on the ideas to address it.

The origins of the "white paper" can be traced back to England in the early 20th century when the British Parliament used it as short research reports. Instead of the blue cover used for other reports, they use the same white paper as the text—sounding a bit aesthetic minimalist—hence the nickname "white papers."

Many governments have since used the term to refer to documents summarizing policies or authoritative reports.

It wasn't until the mid-1990s that "white papers" came into use in corporate marketing, often written by designers familiar with their products. Although it looks like an owner's manual, it tends to be less bombastic than a brochure and more focused on persuasive facts.

Satoshi Nakamoto drafted the first recognized "white paper" for the blockchain. In 2008, the mysterious figure released a technical document on the Internet titled "Bitcoin: A Peer-to-Peer Electronic Cash System."

Nakamoto's close followers refer to this 12-chapter nine pager as Bitcoin's "white paper." The reference meets no controversy among the fans of decentralization worldwide.

However, when launching their ICOs, subsequent projects often borrowed the term to entice the public with many self-justifying, carelessly scribbled "white papers" filled with garbage without the slightest hint of fundamental business ideas.

80 Regulatory Sandbox

Perfect "decentralization" always seems to strive for a brand-new world. But the real world can only be built on intertwined interests and complex human nature. It's more like a middle ground, for whose territory ideals and reality compete in a constant tug-of-war.

Therefore, to explore the possibility of building a new world, "decentralization" must pass the examination in the real world. One of the means is "regulation."

Sandboxing has always been a security mechanism in the field of computer security. When some programs cannot be directly determined to have a specific intention and may have a destructive capacity, people throw them into an experimental environment to run and observe them in isolation. It's like the situation in which a mother who is worrying that her naughty children will cover the room with sand creates a self-contained and isolated sandbox for the little rascals to play.

The British financial regulators invented the regulatory sandbox in 2015. It doesn't directly stifle some initiatives in the financial innovation

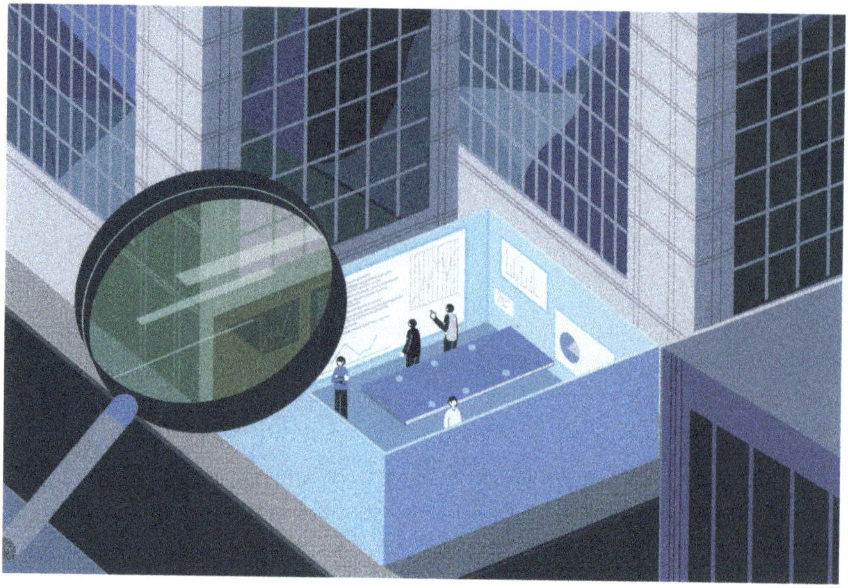

environment. But it remains so prudent that it experiments with these new proposals in an environment disconnected from the whole financial system.

It recruits users and conducts a small-scale pilot with limited freedom. After thoroughly evaluating the test results, it is up to the regulatory authorities to decide whether to officially allow innovative products or services to enter the financial market.

Many countries have used the regulatory model to regulate ICOs. How will this subversive financing model fare in the challenging real world? Is it a prophetic vision, as its proponents claim, or a sheer hoax, as its opponents insist? Regulators in these countries have taken a relatively cautious and open-minded approach.

However, there is a lot of controversy over whether the regulatory sandbox applies to the blockchain. Launching pilot projects in part of the network is a good idea. Blockchain is a new field of knowledge lacking broad social consensus for the time being, and its underlying technical infrastructure is seriously insufficient. It's difficult for start-ups to find users willing to cooperate with the pilot projects under this circumstance. Even if the test results are good, it won't be easy to rig regulators of their concerns about whether it applies to actual financial conditions.

As early as May 2017, China's first government-led sandbox program was unveiled in Guiyang. The most important part is establishing and continuously improving the "Blockchain ICO Sandbox Project." At about the same time, Ganzhou City, Jiangxi Province, also launched the Blockchain Supervision Sandbox Industrial Park. But tightening regulations eventually ended both sandboxes.

81 DAO

Let's put aside the decentralized thinking you've developed with great effort and reflect on how Bitcoin would have been set up if it were treated as a "listed company?"

From the very beginning of its birth, Bitcoin had developed a corporate regulation: a "company provided services for cryptocurrency transactions, and anyone who could acquire bitcoins by purchasing them as they do with stocks could become this "company's" shareholders.

The miners were equivalent to the company's employees, who would work themselves extremely hard to mine and get bitcoin rewards. Unlike the current "996" or even the "007" system of capitalist exploitation of employees, the regulations had long stated that those who work the hardest would get the most rewards so that they became the "company's" shareholders.

With regulations never to be tampered with while having no boss, the company would see employees who recognized the company's rules consciously abide by them.

Some Internet companies implement plans to allow their employees to own stocks because, in this way, every employee will expect the stocks in his hands to appreciate early, so he is willing to work hard to improve the company's performance. Then, the "shareholders" of the Bitcoin network would also try their best to expand the "company."

The above logic of constructing a Bitcoin company describes a typical DAO, which is short for Decentralized Autonomous Organization.

In this Bitcoin "company" with neither a "boss" nor a centralized "board of directors," every "shareholder" enjoys the right to participate in its decision-making process and operation. Meanwhile, the "production," "trade," and bookkeeping" of the "products" are all undertaken by the miners as the company's "employees."

The DAO concept has gone beyond the utopian imagination, thanks to the development of blockchain technology and the emergence of smart contracts.

Blockchain technology has given rise to the autonomy of allowing everyone to participate in DAO, thus ensuring that the operating rules are not manipulated in black boxes. In that case, smart contracts enable DAO to have an intelligent mind to operate independently by following all the set rules.

It's regrettable for the malpractice of stealing what is entrusted to occur from time to time in financial systems worldwide. But in a perfect DAO organization, there is no need to worry that an institution will overissue currency or that perpetrators will tamper with your digital assets. The mushrooming of smart contracts can significantly extend the blockchain application to more aspects of people's lives. Therefore, devout believers in technology supremacy are always willing to imagine a future world full of DAOs.

82 The DAO

The decentralization-embracing DAOs are experiments on creating a new world through cryptocurrency and blockchain technology.

The DAO and DAO sound similar and confusing. In reality, the former is one of the many DAOs. The name with the definite article "the" demonstrates an ambition to be a model for all the DAOs. Like many of them, The DAO is also a DApp on the Ethereum network.

But since its early creation, members of this organization have recognized that the challenges posed by distributed governance far exceed expectations, and The DAO has gone through a vast and complex test in its actual implementation of the DAO's philosophy.

You already learned from the organizational form of DAO before that there is no unequal power relationship in a decentralized ecology because everyone is a co-builder of this ecology. It's also the project philosophy of The DAO, which acts as something like the funds we're dealing with daily.

Fund managers determine traditional funds. For example, they put the raised funds into various investment and financial management "baskets" to work for the appreciation of the customers' assets. But customers who have purchased funds can neither interfere with investment strategies nor detect some fund managers' professional integrity.

The DAO seemed to compete with Wall Street when it first emerged. It intended to defeat this traditional "black-box" investment model and enabled a set of decentralized open rules, returning power to customers.

If you time-travel back to April 30, 2016, you can read the news that The DAO is going ICO on the internet. You find that you only need to pay ether coins to buy The DAO's Token, treating The DAO as a fund, and the Token is equivalent to its share.

Those who have acquired the Token have become The DAO's shareholders, with the right to submit proposals for investment projects directly and vote on the investment proposals being implemented, with one Token equaling a vote. The community decides how The DAO allocates investment in the end.

You may be immediately drawn to this unprecedented transparent system. Because merely 15 days after the ICO opened, the project had raised more than 100 million US dollars. When the fundraising window closed on the 28th day, you had accumulated nearly 15% of the ether coins in circulation on the entire network, like many others beating the rest of the rivals. These ether coins are hosted in The DAO's smart contracts.

But soon, the other side of decentralization bore its ferocious teeth.

A hacker noticed the smart contract hoarding large amounts of ether coins only a month later. He successfully stole as much as 3.6 million coins by exploiting a bug in the smart contract code. You must know that this figure is close to one-third of the crowdfunded ether coins.

This fierce attack itself didn't mean the collapse of the Ethereum ecosystem. It was like a technical hiccup preventing a website from launching that can't be counted as the failure of the entire Internet. However, The DAO, which had a good beginning, had no idea what was in store later: This serious hack permanently changed the whole Ethereum ecosystem.

The hacker's atrocity shocked all the Ethereum participants, who soon discovered the address he had deposited the 3.6 million ether coins. With so many wrathful eyes fixed upon them, the hacker found it hard to withdraw them and take flight.

Some key figures proposed that every fund increase be recorded on the Ethereum blockchain since the raised ether coins were entrusted to the smart contracts. If the coins were stolen at the 10,000th block, all the blocks up to the 9999th still had the record of the amount before the theft. Therefore, if a hard fork were initiated at the 9999th block, the new value formed after that would have no record of the hacker stealing the 3.6 million ether coins in the chain, and the new chain wouldn't recognize all future transactions of this asset.

They calculated that, as long as the old chain didn't have enough computing power support, it would eventually become an abandoned chain, although the old chain still had the record of this theft.

However, many opponents rose in the Ethereum ecosystem to oppose the suggestion. They believed that since it's a decentralized blockchain, there should be no human interference for any reason, not even in the name of justice and morality. They thought people must accept the brute fact of losing the coins. So they remained on the old chain instead of switching their computing power to support the establishment of a new chain.

Two chains eventually coexist due to this Ethereum's hard fork: One is a new one called Ethereum, created to recover stolen ether coins, and the other is the old chain backed by miners who didn't leave the battlefield for others.

It's called Ethereum Classic.

In fact, this currency-stealing incident has another far-reaching impact: Many people have discovered that there was the possibility of having factors of instability on the Ethereum network, the ecology loaded with countless DApps. A loophole in any smart contract may cause systemic turmoil as long as hackers steal enough ether coins. Because of this, however, the Ethereum community has learned to be more prudent. Hackers may never stop doing evil, but community members have also reached an unwritten agreement to restrain from initiating a hard fork due to theft.

83 DAS

A future world full of DAOs, also known as DAS (Decentralized Autonomous Society), extends the concept of autonomous organizations to social forms' construction.

It's a great and novel proposition but also a whim at the same time.

You wake up one morning only to find your digital assets equivalent to 3,000 yuan automatically deducted from your authorized cryptocurrency wallet. You've transferred the funds to the landlord despite how much the rent will inflate when this assumption becomes a reality. If you annul the authorization, the lock to your door won't recognize the private key you've used to sign the contract, and you'll be refused entrance.

Similarly, if the landlord closes the account used to pay property tax to

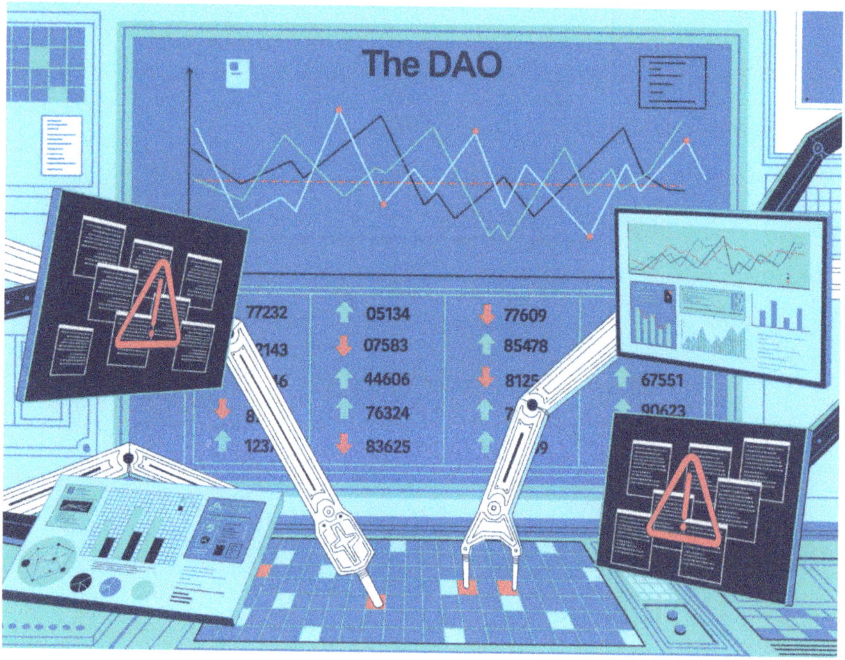

the government, he will also lose the apartment's ownership. The original sale and purchase contract will be automatically switched to the government, which will become your new landlord.

You can see your donated cryptocurrency recorded on the blockchain and end up in a charity account used to help the children in the mountainous area or the account of a research institute studying the methods of prolonging human lifespan from 170 to 200 years.

You decide to go to work in that self-driving car produced not by a large-size 21st-century automobile factory but by a genuine DAO.

You follow the choices made by the car's algorithm. You may waste 11 more minutes bypassing an expensive toll road but receive some fees from the drivers to whom you've yielded the right of way on the expressway. You also find a business opportunity to earn some pocket money as you listen to the radio broadcast on your way and bring some goods from a warehouse to a customer who lives at your destination.

In 30 minutes, you've paid cryptocurrency equivalent to 9 yuan and toll to 10. Meanwhile, you've received 10 yuan from yielding the right of the way and a tip of 30 for goods delivery.

In DAS, you can freely offer any service you want at your fingertips and earn cryptocurrency directly from it. Of course, you can also post requirements anytime, anywhere, which will become your way of life.

The above scenario is from the vision of Vitalik Buterin, the Father of Ethereum, and I've only localized it. He has outlined DAS, or we can

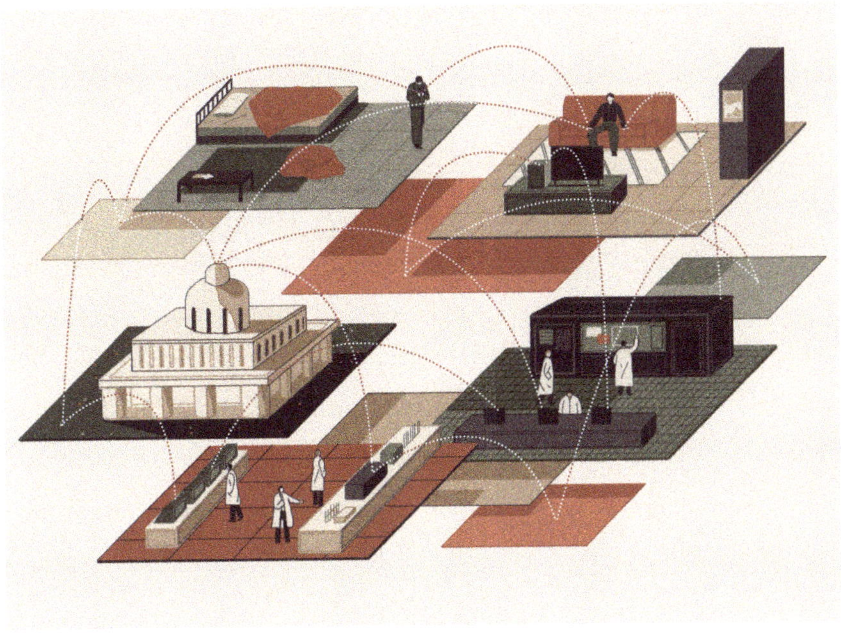

understand it as a description of the potential of a blockchain to reshape the world.

Avid geeks welcome it enthusiastically, looking forward eagerly to seeing the present human society reshaped by computer science with its cold technologies and codes.

Of course, many people claim that it's but a utopian fantasy. The story's protagonists are like living on a desert island on the high seas, escaping from the existing world like the drifting Robinson Crusoe.

No one seems confident enough to make judgments now, but DAS is a possibility of gradual evolution. Where there are changes, there're also shifting opportunities.

84 Cypherpunks

When you hear the term "punks," what you see in your mind's eye may be exaggerated tattoos and boots or a smoldering derelict boat covered in graffiti. But you probably have never heard about cypherpunks. They don't party underground, chanting proclamations of personal liberation over frenzied rock music. But they are mostly a bunch of taciturn tech nerds.

Instead of producing glamorous works of performance art, these hard-core geeks claiming to defend individual consciousness with cryptography cherish no fewer ideals than the real-world punks.

The average person had never heard about cryptography before the 1970s because it was only a military intelligence tool locked behind forbidden government office doors.

In the late 1980s, whether encryption technology should be strictly controlled or set free suddenly sparked a frenzy of discussion among Americans. The civilianization of the Internet in the 1990s finally lifted the last mysterious veil of this technology.

A retired physicist invited more than two dozen friends to his home to discuss cryptography and citizens' privacy in 1992. Later, this private gathering gradually evolved into a monthly company meeting. One person in the group humorously called these people "cypherpunks."

In *A Cypherpunks Manifesto*, published a year later, the extreme advocates in this organization declared to the public, "Privacy is necessary for an open society in the electronic age.... We cannot expect governments, corporations, or other large, faceless organizations to grant us privacy out of their beneficence.... We must defend our own privacy if we expect to have any."

Around the same time, one of the organization's founders compiled an encrypted mailing list known as the "Cypherpunks Mailing List." The cypherpunks compared notes freely via this private circle by receiving encrypted emails. Their discussion ranged from cryptography and computer science's coding philosophy to the political and economic ecology of the time.

The cypherpunks' ranks continued to expand, and most members were IT elites. They included Julian Assange, founder of WikiLeaks; Tim Berners-Lee, WWW invertor; Nick Szabo, initiator of the smart contract concept; Sean Parker, one of the Facebook founders; and Satoshi Nakamoto, who later created Bitcoin.

Satoshi Nakamoto's *The White Paper*, which we mentioned earlier, was first posted on the "Cypherpunks Mailing List." Bitcoin's features, such as decentralization and privacy of anonymity, all represent the cypherpunks' spirit.

In fact, members of this organization had discussed and published at least ten cryptocurrencies and cryptocurrency systems before the appearance of Bitcoin. For example, David Chaum launched E-cash in 1993, while Wei Dai proposed B-money in 1998. They might have failed, but Bitcoin rose upon these giants' shoulders.

For instance, the spirit of Bitcoin at the core is "anonymity of transactions" and the P2P network. Both were found in B-money. The PoW consensus mechanisms originated from the cypherpunks Adam Back and Hal Finney, who later became fans of Bitcoin and gave Satoshi Nakamoto many suggestions on its design and revision.

It's fair to say that Bitcoin is Satoshi Nakamoto's masterpiece. But I prefer to regard it as a gift to this world from the cypherpunks' trend of thought.

85 "100 Million Yuan Pizzas"

The Bitcoin community comprises the most consensus-oriented people on the planet, and their consensus is celebrated as "Bitcoin Pizza Day " every May 27. Many cryptocurrency enthusiasts share with their friends that day pizza photos with bitcoin-related elements.

The association of Bitcoin with pizzas started in May 2010.

On May 18 of that year, an American programmer named Laszlo Hanyecz posted on the BitcoinTalk, a Bitcoin forum, claiming that he was willing to spend 10,000 bitcoins to buy two pizzas and posted the address where he would receive the pizzas to be delivered to him. At that time, bitcoin transactions were mere self-entertaining activities only among Bitcoin geeks. Laszlo accidentally became the first geek in the history of Bitcoin

transactions to "venture out of the circle."

On May 22, Laszlo updated his post, stating that he had completed the transaction with a guy from the UK named "Jercos," whose real name is Jeremy Sturdivant, and attached a picture of the pizzas. The price of the two pizzas was $25, with an exchange rate of 0.25 cents per bitcoin.

The post was recovered after it hadn't been heard about for a long time. People began to leave comments one after another. Some even set up Twitter accounts to record the current prices of the two pizzas.

Especially in December 2017, when the price of a bitcoin approached $20,000, the anecdote of the pizza sale seven years before was sensationalized. At that time, the two pizzas were worth over 100 million yuan, thus creating the legend of "100 million yuan pizzas."

The current "Bitcoin Pizza Day" is not only a cultural totem to commemorate this dramatic event but also a gathering to recharge the global cryptocurrency community's faith.

Laszlo Hanyecz owned so many bitcoins back then because he had become a hard-core follower of Bitcoin long before. He had started mining with a more efficient GPU when other miners still used their desktops' CPUs. He mined around a few thousand bitcoins daily.

Someone has kept statistics based on a Bitcoin address published by Laszlo since the transaction records of bitcoins are transparent throughout the network. After purchasing the two pizzas, he has successively sold 80,000 bitcoins, almost depleting his bitcoin account.

He admitted that some people became wealthy after buying bitcoins from him. This first geek who verified the property of Bitcoin currency transactions has claimed with a laughing-himself tone that he had never regretted what he had done.

"Jercos," the other protagonist of the same story, who had bought 10,000 bitcoins for only $25, sold them out for $400 as early as 2011.

86 The Mt. Gox Scandal

Mt. Gox is known to Chinese cryptocurrency enthusiasts by its homonym, Mentougou, a district of Beijing, the capital of China. It was one of the thousands of cryptocurrency exchanges not worth our pen and ink. However, since its glory and demise have left us valuable lessons to learn and reflect upon, it's worth our pause to learn about its trajectory.

Mt. Gox was once the largest cryptocurrency exchange in the world, headquartered in Shibuya, Tokyo, Japan. It was responsible for 70% of the global bitcoin trading volume in 2013 but declared bankruptcy in 2014.

The Mt. Gox website was originally an online platform Jed McCaleb developed for a tradable card game called Magic: The Gathering Online. It was abbreviated from the name of the service, Magic: The Gathering Online exchange.

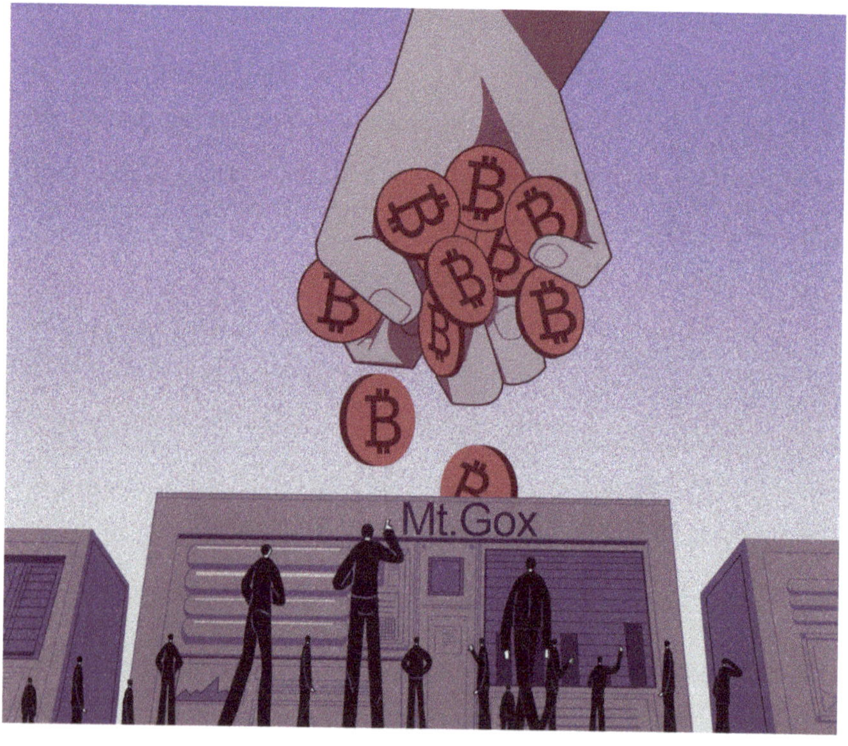

Jed McCaleb transformed the website into a Bitcoin exchange in 2010 and sold it to Bitcoin enthusiast Mark Karpeles the following year.

Mt. Gox had been hacked many times before it became the world's largest bitcoin trading platform. However, the bitcoins worth a few million US dollars lost to the "petty thieves" were ignored due to the thriving trend of bitcoin trading.

This institution had the mission of "changing the world's financial order" in the eyes of its believers. However, it took a turn for the worse beginning in 2013. At first, it was sued by a partnership for $75 million. Then, by the end of the year, BTC China, another cryptocurrency exchange, had surpassed its average daily trading volume.

The fatal blow came in February of the following year. Mt. Gox announced that it suspended all Bitcoin services due to "technical problems." User panic caused the price of a bitcoin to drop abruptly from $800 to $100.

Two weeks later, an internal document leaked from the exchange's website, claiming that it was hit by an unprecedented case of theft, losing as many as 744,408 bitcoins worth about $350 million.

Mt. Gox was soon declared bankrupt. The strange trajectory of its downward spiral since 2013 aroused the suspicion and wrath of its users, who had suffered tremendous losses. Hackers attacked its trading system successively, exposing more and more of the company's malpractices, including mismanagement of the company, insider trading, and suspected fraud. They found tons of bitcoins missing, and the discovery triggered floods of criticism against Mt. Gox for stealing what the users had entrusted to its care. Mark Karpeles, the CEO of Mt. Gox, was arrested on charges of embezzlement and misappropriation of the company's funds.

Even today, the Mt. Gox scandal remains a rare case of exchange theft. The most paradoxical thing is that a centralized trading platform never seems able to undertake the heavy task of building a decentralized trading ecosystem.

The scandal reveals the evil of "pseudo-decentralized institutions, and the deviltry is even worse than the so-called financial dignitaries once objected to by blockchain believers. Criminal forces are always surging stealthily though so many people are striving to break out of the centralized world. Many theft cases have occurred in exchanges worldwide since the Mt. Gox scandal.

87 "Tulip"

Suppose the early understanding of blockchain and cryptocurrencies was analogous to a draft of thought drifting alone. In that case, a pack of terrifying "specters" has always been trying to interfere with its course. They are the profound fears people have had of repeated financial scams. Among them, the "Tulip" is a well-known symbol that opponents of Bitcoin often mention with bitcoins in the same breath.

Around 1636, a frenzy about tulips swept the Netherlands, where the plant's bulbs became a hot "currency." One bulb could exchange for eight fat pigs, four plump cows, two tons of butter, 1,000 pounds of cheese, a silver

cup, a bag of clothes, a bed, and a boat.

The frenzy seemed to have many similarities with that of Bitcoin. Tulips had just been introduced to Europe then and coincided with the beginning of the Netherlands' golden age. The vibrance and glory are visible in the light and shades of Rembrandt's paintings. As people were eager to invest their capital, business-minded Dutch tumbled into a big gamble.

A scenario of Bitcoin's deflationary expectations occurred. Initially, the expensive bulbs were rare varieties only. But due to their short supply, the common plant species' bulbs also started to sell well. It was nothing like the ICO explosion around 2017 when numerous cryptocurrencies without intrinsic values soon followed suit.

Many opponents of Bitcoin believe it's nothing but strings of numbers and letters. When bitcoins were exchanged for real objects for the first time in 2010, each coin was worth $0.03 only. It reached $20,000 because the frenzy was similar to the Netherlands' tulip mania.

The "Tulip mania" has been used as a metaphor for any giant economic bubble in which the price of an asset deviates from its intrinsic value. The speculators eager to get rich overnight during Bitcoin's surge repeated the Dutch's madness. More and more critics say that Bitcoin is like the burst bubbles of the tulips, with the price plummeting to one percent of its original value overnight.

However, it may not be wise to use the tulip tragedy to predict Bitcoin's fate. The fundamental problem was that even the rarest tulip bulbs couldn't guarantee their property of rarity at that time. The aesthetic trend inflating their prices was more likely to recede over time. It has been guaranteed in the code from the beginning that no more bitcoins would be issued. Even the set rhythm of mining has been programmed so that no external force, not even the hidden hand of God, can influence its rarity.

88 Mainchain and Sidechain

The sidechain is a concept relative to the parent blockchain, or mainchain. Suppose Ethereum is regarded as a mainchain. Let's examine a sidechain and how it constructs a set of game rules.

Now, imagine some DApps on Ethereum that offer streaming movies. The developers and maintainers of those DApps quickly discovered a problem: It would be ridiculously expensive to host the films on Ethereum. The cost of storing a transaction with 1MB of data on the chain is as costly as thousands of yuan, and the file sizes of high-definition movies are all in GB.

The Ethereum network isn't good at storing huge data. People then thought of developing a sidechain by copying Ethereum's open-source code with slight modifications to optimize it for large file storage. A public blockchain was thus born. The developers subsequently rented a bunch of servers to provide nodes for miners, even though the number was still small compared with Ethereum at first.

For now, we may call this chain a "movie chain" and the cryptocurrency used as rewards "movie currency." The developers initially wanted to build a proprietary chain for storing "big-size" data, a goal they have already achieved. Compared with Ethereum, the "movie chain" has given up many of its functions, thereby improving its storage efficiency and reducing the cost of working on the chain.

At this stage, the "movie chain" looked like a copy of the Ethereum blockchain. But don't worry! The story is only beginning. The developers hope to connect the "movie chain's" ecosystem with Ethereum. For example, users with "movie coins" can quickly watch movies on Ethereum's DApps. To make this happen, the developers enable the users to go to the exchange to sell their "movie coins" and purchase ethers to spend. But it doesn't have to be so complicated if the "movie chain" uses the smart contract with added cross-chain technology, allowing users of the "movie chain" and Ethereum to conduct P2P currency exchange.

However, the "movie chain" still has a problem. It doesn't have enough nodes, the degree of its decentralization is low, and users aren't eager to participate. How to improve the chain's ecosystem, then?

Now, smart contracts come into play, binding all transactions occurring on the "movie chain" to Ethereum. The records of the stored movies and "movie coins'" transaction details can be plugged into the Ethereum network, which can boost the credibility of the sidechain.

The lofty vision of the "movie chain" is that the function of decentralized storage of huge amounts of data can attract increasingly more users. Simultaneously, they also hope that the "movie coin's" price will soar, the new miners' number will increase, and movie-related DApps will be released on the chain.

That is the trajectory of the sidechain's rise from something of less consequence.

In reality, Ethereum has no idea how many sidechains it has. Many blockchains have been designed as Ethereum's sidechains to enhance their sense of value recognition. They are mostly used to store and compute huge amounts of data.

In contrast, Bitcoin only owns some experimental sidechains and hasn't become a scale ecosystem. The fundamental reason is that Bitcoin's script function is limited, and its own "currency" DNA determines that it's difficult to carry and extend such rich application logic.

89 Cross-Chain Technology

Instead of a chain, cross-chain is a technology that provides value transfer between two or more blockchains. For example, it can play a significant role in the instance of the movie DApp we cited when explaining the sidechain.

The sidechain uses its unique Token. Now, suppose you're an ether holder. Suppose you want to use the movie copyright stored on this sidechain. In that case, you must first exchange your ether coins for the Token used in the sidechain ecosystem. That's because the sidechain uses cross-chain technology, greatly facilitating currency-to-currency conversion.

The whole process is like this: When you request to exchange one ether coin for 10,000 sidechain tokens, the smart contract with enabled cross-chain technology will help you find and match people who accept your offer on the chain. After the match is successful, the cross-chain technology ensures that your withdrawals are completely simultaneous, and neither party will take risks due to time lapses.

As we said before, sidechain tokens can also be listed on exchanges, but you may be wondering why you can't buy them directly from exchanges. The reason is that many fans of decentralization distrust centralized exchanges after all. Then, you may ask if purchasing cryptocurrencies from decentralized exchanges is feasible.

Decentralized exchanges use cross-chain technology for currency transactions. The entire trade matching and the process mentioned above are precisely the same. Decentralized exchanges automatically use smart contracts to match transactions between buyers and sellers and employ cross-chain technology to exchange currencies securely.

Achieving decentralized transactions is itself the main mission of cross-chain technology.

The user-friendly exchange between currencies makes the application of DApps more appealing. Suppose you possess a bunch of bitcoins in your wallet but want to rent a house using a DApp built on the Ethereum network. But the experience would be lousy when you must first exchange bitcoins for ethers or the tokens from the exchange's DApp if it doesn't have the cross-chain technology.

With the blessing of cross-chain technology, things would be different: When you open the front end of a DApp, which may be a web page or an app, you'll most likely see many other digital currencies supported at the payment portal. The scenario resembles the situation where you make payments on the Internet and see it supporting WeChat, Alipay, bank cards, and other methods. Suppose a real estate rental DApp is regarded as a provider of application services. In that case, behind every accepted digital currency is a payment DApp service supported by cross-chain technology. Transaction information between chains can communicate with each other under the cross-chain framework.

Did you see that the experience of using DApps is akin to the apps to which we're so customized? It also allows the three-dimensional penetration of blockchain applications to leave more room for imagination.

That's not the ending of the cross-chain technology story. It isn't a mere tool for completing decentralized transactions. It can also help achieve logical divisions of labor in centralized organizational structures. For example, a listed company can build multiple private chains, enjoys its procurement chain, boasts its auditing chain, and communicate across various chains. Simultaneously, it can ensure privacy by opening only the audit chain's data to audit institutions.

90 Protocol Layer and Application Layer

If the Internet is regarded as a layered model, it can be roughly divided into the protocol and application layers. Network operators and equipment manufacturers such as China Telecom and Huawei belong to the protocol layer, with their value lying primarily in providing infrastructure services. On the other hand, Internet companies like Tencent and Alibaba belong to the application layer, creating practical application scenarios and ecosystems for end users.

This way of describing hierarchical structures also applies to blockchains. You may assume that the protocol layer projects are responsible for "building roads" for blockchains, whereas the application layer projects are the cars

speeding on them. For example, Ethereum belongs to the protocol layer, and DApps created through the underlying protocols it provides can be classified into the application layer.

The relationship between the application and protocol layers is organic. DApp users don't feel the protocol layer's existence. It's as if you browse the web without knowing how the underlying TCP/IP (Transmission Control Protocol/Internet Protocol) protocols work.

However, unlike the situation where most brilliant Internet superstars or influencers come from the application layer, the protocol layer accounts for a much larger proportion of the blockchain projects currently recognized by market values than the application layer. The protocol layer brings more financial returns for start-up entrepreneurs, resulting in more cryptocurrency values.

Let's first examine why the Internet's application-layer projects can make money. It would be as difficult as ascending to the sky if you wanted to copy a star project like Facebook, wouldn't it? That's because it possesses a massive amount of user data, which has formed an invincible "moat" to protect this "commercial castle." The cost of creating another Facebook is unimaginable.

The blockchain today, however, has broken the data monopoly. Give some free rein to your imagination. If Facebook were a blockchain project comparable to distributed data storage on a public network, would it be easier to create a similar social media network through a hard fork? In other words, the blockchain application layer project doesn't have a so-called commercial "moat" to depress its estimated market value.

People were more aware of the blockchain protocol layer's unique value, at least in the early stages of the industry, because an application-layer project, no matter how excellent, will ultimately depend strongly on a protocol layer supported by enough miners. Think about it. Does the essence of the blockchain application value lie in building trust? Then, what's the foundation of trust? Don't you think sufficient nodes are bolstering it? Obviously, a blockchain network with many nodes is always more secure and reliable than a network with few. As a result, protocol layer projects always have a stronger sense of existence in the current blockchain world.

However, this situation may change in the future. An excellent application layer project may develop its own protocol layer and build a basic network.

91 Sharding

A technology used by ordinary databases, sharding isn't unique to the blockchain. In the past, all data was stored in one database, the drawbacks of which are evident. Constantly increasing data amount decreases the performance, not conducive to data management and access query.

Sharding divides a massive database into small chunks, scattering and storing them in different shards. Each shard has unique data not to be shared with the data in other shards.

The connotation of sharding is extended when it's applied to the blockchain.

Developers have tried their utmost to alleviate network congestion. One of their results is the sharding technology.

The main job of nodes is to accept and verify transactions and forward them to the blockchain ledger in the original blockchain network. Each node handles all the work in the network at the same time. The so-called "congestion" increases transaction volume, causing nodes to be overwhelmed.

Sharding divides the blockchain network into multiple instances, and the data is distributed and arranged in different instances for processing. These shards work in parallel, and each node doesn't have to load the entire network's data but only the information in the shard for which it is responsible.

Take transaction information as an example. You publish a transaction initially to be verified, forwarded, and stored by the miners of the entire network. Now, with the sharding technology, your transaction may be divided into certain instances per specific rules, such as your transaction ID's last digit, and processed by the nodes in this instance. As a result, the entire network can process more transactions simultaneously.

Suppose 10,000 people are making robots together, and everyone is required to make one on his own and see who finishes the first in the end. This method would waste so many people's energy and repeated labor. If these people were divided into various teams, with some responsible for manufacturing the arms and others making the legs, then the efficiency of the entire process would be significantly enhanced.

However, there is a clear industrial division of labor in manufacturing robots from the beginning, and there will be no "conflict" in working procedures. On the virtual blockchain network, it's necessary to consider real-time cross-instance and cross-server communications.

For example, suppose you bought a cup of coffee with a bitcoin, and this transaction is distributed to Instance 1. Almost simultaneously, you bought a cake with the same coin distributed to Instance 2. Since only one of these two transactions is valid, instant communication between Instances 1 and 2 is necessary. Otherwise, no one would know that the transactions are conflicting in the network. Such a case is called "cross-shard protocol."

92 Hyperledger

Hyperledger is an open-source project led by the Linux Foundation. You can treat it as a whole set of modules that can be plugged in and out instantly to help you quickly create a consortium blockchain system. You don't have to waste time and energy creating the chain if you want to use it to develop a consortium blockchain. You only need to divert your energy to developing smart contracts on it.

We can imagine ourselves in the scenario of a consortium blockchain and see how Hyperledger works.

Let's say you're now an IT worker at an automotive original equipment manufacturer (OEM). You know very well that OEMs belong to the downstream sectors, and the upstream sectors are connected to many partners. For example, tire manufacturers supply them to OEMs, manufacturers of wheels provide them to the tire manufacturers, and the wheel manufacturers must purchase aluminum ingots as the raw material to make the wheels.

You may have heard complaints at company meetings like this: The fund settlement cycle height is uncertain due to too many partners and prolonged logistics time. During actual operations, the various manufacturing units waste time, labor, and money on repeated and redundant communications, confirmations, and signatures. Your boss becomes impatient and calls you into his office, where he blurts out the term "blockchain."

You know that partner enterprises belong to the same business network. Suppose a consortium blockchain can be built to connect them as interlinked nodes. In that case, each transaction will be safely recorded on the chain. You find that your boss's idea of trying to save the cost of communication and settlement with the upstream and downstream sectors does make sense. But the question is where to start with such a gigantic IT project.

You find that Hyperledger has built a complete set of the underlying framework of the consortium blockchain. The infrastructure projects such as consensus and communication are also "in place." Issues like data backup and server stability are also taken into consideration. Using this set of "modules," you don't have to worry about developing a chain.

Your next task is creating a smart contract closer to the industrial ecosystem. For example, a wheel manufacturer may not want other partners to know the price it has offered to an OEM. It's up to you to determine which

nodes have the right to know which part of the information.

Before everything starts, you can select the sub-projects best fitting your company's needs from Hyperledger's project database. The best-known Fabric, one of the ledgers, is more like a general-purpose framework, and some sub-projects can provide more precise infrastructure in some sub-areas.

93 BaaS

The letter "B" refers to "blockchain," and the abbreviated "aaS" comprises the first letters of "as a Service." BaaS refers to how services are provided to customers through a cloud computing platform. For example, SaaS (Software as a Service) provides cloud software services for users.

As you know, enterprise-level software is generally expensive, easily costing a company hundreds of thousands of dollars yearly. It isn't cost-effective to purchase the right of use if an enterprise doesn't use it very often. With the SaaS technology, software providers can deploy it on the cloud-computing platform. Without downloading the software locally, enterprises can use it while it's on the cloud-computing platform. The cost is reduced with the pay-as-you-use scheme.

BaaS (Blockchain as a Service) means blockchain-coordinated services provided to enterprise users through cloud computing platforms. This way, they can quickly develop and manage their blockchains at a low cost. This kind of service is generally related to consortium blockchain, and the "template" that BaaS provides is Hyperledger.

Let's assume you're now a baby formula company's CEO. Since the product is a sensitive topic in public opinion polls due to the 2008 milk scandal in China, you want to make the supply chain of this industry transparent. This way, the public can trace the sources of raw materials while

Part 5 Past Events and Present Tense

the industry's upstream and downstream sections can supervise and endorse each other.

But you and other conscientious co-workers soon discover that deploying a blockchain requires a lot of computer equipment that is costly to acquire and maintain. What's worse, you must have a team with blockchain development skills. You shake your head helplessly after pondering the controversial comments on blockchains permeating the Internet and the various hidden costs of deploying a blockchain.

Fortunately, you don't have to take all the trouble. You can use the Hyperledger template to generate your consortium blockchain with the click of a button as long as you prepare your business logic before writing it into a smart contract installable on a BaaS-provided platform and select a configuration that suits your needs.

With the chain deployed on a cloud server, you can access and manage blockchain data on the cloud platform. Meanwhile, the BaaS provider maintains the server. Your developers don't have to know the blockchain details.

In fact, this can be compared to some expensive outdoor outfits.

For example, a scuba diver needs such equipment as a pair of goggles, a buoyancy compensator, a diving dress, and a diver instrument. Their purchase, maintenance, and repair can easily cost thousands of dollars, which is a lot of money for a hobbyist. Therefore, many players who dive infrequently won't buy their equipment. They rent the most suitable equipment from shops near the diving site. These diving outfit shops generally have equipment of various styles to choose from and provide related diver-supporting services, such as renting boats and providing route guidance.

94 USDT

If Bitcoin, which enjoys the highest public recognition, is qualified to be called the "price anchor," then the Tether company that issues and manipulates USDT (Tether USD) comprises a team of careerists dreaming of becoming the "value anchors" of the trading market.

Tether planned to create a value-stable cryptocurrency as an intermediary for currency transactions. USDT is what it has done. The price of USDT is pegged to USD 1:1. Suppose you exchange one bitcoin for 2,000 USDT priced as one bitcoin to USD 2,000 today. You can trade 2,000 USDT at this price anytime in the future. USDT is exchanged for $2,000 worth of bitcoins.

Traders, especially frequent traders, have welcomed it. They prefer to exchange fiat currency or other cryptocurrencies for USDT and store them in their trading accounts. USDT is a stable trading chip that can withstand the risk of cryptocurrency's value plummeting.

You can imagine that you've got five kilograms of rice and want to exchange them for your neighbor's calf. However, the neighbor refuses to trade his calf for rice. Instead, he wants 2.5 kilograms of potatoes, the most sought-after at present. But you had just switched your rice with potatoes

when ten tons of the same vegetable was shipped to town, causing its price to plummet. Under this circumstance, you have to topple your neighbor's fence and leave the 2.5 kilograms of potatoes in his backyard. He has to drive you away, shaking his head.

You regret not exchanging your rice for RMB before using it to buy the calf.

In this fiction, the potatoes are as good as the volatile cryptocurrency, whereas the RMB yuan resembles the stablecoin, the ideal medium of trade.

The design of USDT sounds wonderful, but the story is far from that simple.

USDT's logic makes sense because it makes ensuring price stability its prerequisite. So, how does the Tether company safeguard the stability of USDT's price? The mystery it claims is linking it with gold, as the U.S. did when it pegged its dollar issuance to gold. At that time, the U.S. Federal Reserve promised that every time a certain amount of U.S. dollars was issued, a corresponding amount of gold would be stored to bolster its value. Tether promises to keep $1.00 of asset reserves in its bank account for each issued USDT, and a USDT will be destroyed every time it is exchanged for a USD.

In other words, Tether Limited uses this method to ensure that the price ratio of USDT and USD is always 1:1. It hopes that the price of USDT will still be considered near-constant though USDT may fluctuate slightly with the USD.

However, the issuance of USD depends on the credibility of the Federal Reserve. People may wonder if Tether can live up to its promises. Users may exchange USDT by remitting their funds to Tether Limited's bank account or purchasing USDT from other users via exchanges. In that case, how will the company ensure the safety of those users' assets? What credibility does it have to give its users peace of mind?

If a centralized company can be ethically flawless, then the so-called core value of blockchain to pursue fairness and transparency will be superfluous.

Tether Limited may think it has blazed the trail by coming up with this idea of creating a medium of exchange. However, under close examination, we can see that it's dancing on the edge of a knife of morality.

In November 2017, $30.95 million worth of USDT was stolen from the Tether Treasury's wallet, causing market panic. Tether Limited arranged for an audit company to intervene in the audit to prove that its bank account assets and USDT issuance are indeed consistent. But this show of its determination to maintain its moral integrity is merely a drop in the bucket.

In early 2018, Tether Limited was accused of hiding things during auditing, and it soon ceased cooperating with the audit company.

Did Tether overissue USDT? The question has since become a mystery in cryptocurrency circles.

USDT's cryptocurrency market value may be the highest in the world. However, it results from many countries' joint efforts to block cryptocurrency exchanges.

In the past, when an exchange provided full trading services, users only needed to deposit fiat currency into the exchange's bank account. But exchanges are under tremendous pressure from banks and regulators after being banned from allowing their users to invest and withdraw fiat money.

The introduction of USDT is as good as opening a gray area. The exchange only provides trade matching services to buyers and sellers of fiat and USDT. That means that the buyers purchase USDT from other users with their fiat money via the exchange, with the funds flowing directly into the bank account of the seller, who then uses the USDT in the exchange's bank account to buy other cryptocurrencies. Financial supervision can be skillfully evaded since fiat money isn't deposited in the exchange's bank account. That's the primary reason for USDT's promotion in recent years.

95 Stablecoin

You must have seen their steep and unpredictable trend curves if you have held cryptocurrencies. However, there is one cryptocurrency that claims to be price stable. In an ideal design model, a "stablecoin" would always have a constant price relative to its anchored currency.

USDT was the first stable currency, but when it was first designed, there was no such a concept as a "stable currency." Inspired by its great success, many imitators have emerged.

You may wonder what has motivated one team after another to dedicate themselves to the creation of this currency since its price can't be hyped.

First, when the user exchanges the stablecoin for fiat currency, that is, when he redeems his fiat currency from the stablecoin development team, he needs to pay the handling fee for the team to destroy the USDT. It's the initial benefit the team gets from developing the stablecoin.

Second, since the stablecoin team has a large amount of fiat currency stored in its bank account, just like other centralized financial institutions, these assets can be used for investment to appreciate their value.

Exchanges have always been the best allies for stablecoins, not only because stablecoins help to avoid financial regulations but also because when fiat currency directly participates in the exchange of cryptocurrencies, it will involve high fees and waiting times for cross-border payments. The introduction of stablecoins is in the interests of exchanges.

Some stablecoins regarded USDT as a classic and maintained the stability of their prices by depositing fiat currency or gold in bank accounts as collateral. But the exposed flaws of centralization quickly gave rise to many repercussions from stablecoin holders, who were increasingly concerned about behind-the-scene manipulations between banks and stablecoin issuers.

As a result, a new stablecoin requiring no banking operations has emerged. This currency is also expected to form a stable price ratio of 1:1 with the USD. The team behind it does not have a bank but a cryptocurrency account. Every time a stablecoin is issued, a proportional ether coin will be deposited in this account accordingly. Since the ledger of Ethereum is transparent and verifiable, doubts about the over-issuance of stablecoins like USDT can be dispelled.

However, as collateral against the stablecoins, ether coins fluctuate relative to the USD. So, how can this stablecoin ensure that its price is always stable? The answer is the principle of developing a smart contract. Users must also exchange stablecoins worth $100. They only have to deposit fewer ether coins when their price rises and more when they fall.

However, for this mechanism to gain public confidence, it must always ensure that at all times, the total value of the ether coins in the account is greater than the full value of the stablecoins. The stablecoins' total value remains equal to the product of its issuance and 1 USD. It can no longer support this market value once the collateral's value is insufficient. It's like you mortgage your house to a bank loan, and the bank must ensure that the real property's total price is within its risk-control range.

Stablecoin development teams have developed over-collateralization mechanisms to gain people's unshakable trust. It means that when you exchange stablecoins worth $100, you must transfer the excess value of your ether coins. The practice guarantees the total value of the ether coins in the entire account to a great extent.

The automatically executed dynamic anchoring mechanism is designed to maintain the price ratio between the stablecoin and the USD. However, the public doesn't quite accept it because this stablecoin's volatility exceeds those directly pegged to fiat money. Besides, the entire mechanism is pretty intricate.

A "wilder" design appeared in the realm of stablecoins, requiring no assets as collateral. Teams of these stablecoins find that USD has long decoupled itself from gold in the real world and that the issuance of fiat money needs no endorsement with commodities. Therefore, they have committed themselves to replicating this reality in blockchain with coding.

This way, this stablecoin relies on code-based algorithms to automatically control the supply of stablecoins, simulating the invisible hand of central banks to regulate the relationship between the supply and demand of money. When the market for this stablecoin exceeds the demand, the stablecoins circulating in the market will be recycled, and vice versa.

However, the money supply is complex because it involves diverse variables in the operation of the real-world economy, so it is easy to imagine how difficult it is to use code to control and adjust currencies. There have been multiple stablecoins of this type that have fallen into a vicious cycle and collapsed completely.

96 Libra

The Goddess of Justice in Greek mythology holds scales in one hand and a saber in the other. Blindfolded, she passes judgment between right and wrong for humans. A few stars form a constellation called Libra, which is related to the myth of this goddess.

Facebook, a U.S. social media platform, refers to the cryptocurrency it designed in 2019 as Libra, drawing on its connotation of "fairness."

Facebook envisions Libra being a borderless cryptocurrency that people can use safely and conveniently in their daily lives. Living in a country like China, where mobile payment is highly developed, we are likely to forget that 2 billion people are still divorced from the modern financial system. Those people without bank accounts may be able to use Libra to make payments in the future without having to endure their countries' terrible financial systems.

Facebook has worked hard to shape this "financial fairness" idea in Libra's white paper.

As a medium of value exchange between people, the Libra cryptocurrency is also designed as a stable currency like USDT, which Facebook will guarantee with real asset reserves to ensure that each Libra issued is backed by a basket of currencies and assets of corresponding value. These assets are primarily cash and government securities provided by less volatile central banks.

According to the white paper, "this borderless cryptocurrency will be launched in 2020. Users can obtain coins on Libra-supporting exchanges, digital wallets, and other platforms. They can also spend their cryptocurrencies in various Libra-supporting applications.

"To mitigate the public's accusation of USDT-initiated "centralization," Libra also claims that the Libra Association will be responsible for maintaining the operation of the entire blockchain, including the asset reserves behind supervision, and promoting the expansion of Libra's financial ecosystem. The Libra Association is a membership organization with members comprising some Internet applications, financial institutions, and telecommunication companies. Facebook is only one of them.

"The development team also tries to strike a commercial balance when choosing a consensus mechanism. It has Libra controlled by a foundation composed of some large nodes at the sacrifice of some attributes of decentralization. It replaces it with a "multi-centralized" form in exchange for the advantage of transaction performance."

There may be indications that this would become a consortium blockchain, but the white paper promised to transform it into a true public blockchain in five years.

The release of the Libra white paper attracted unprecedented attention from all walks of life worldwide, primarily because Facebook has 2.7 billion users. Facebook's move was seen as an "exodus" for cryptocurrency. If a borderless payment carrier materialized, a new financial world that human beings have never seen might appear. At least for a considerable number of people, the overall happiness of the world would increase accordingly.

However, these rebels trying to turn the tide were hit by a strong reaction from the real world. A massive and concerted effort to suppress Libra has brought its creators to the harsh reality.

The most significant obstacle comes from the U.S. government. Mark Zuckerberg, a co-founder of Facebook and chairman of its parent company Meta Platforms, was summoned to Capital Hill several times to answer serious questions from Congress members concerned that his move would weaken USD's dominance. They asked Facebook to cease developing and promoting Libra regardless that USD accounted for the largest share of the reserve assets behind Libra.

Libra opponents also worried that Libra could create financial risks and be used for money laundering and terrorism financing. Other countries were also aware of the threat that Libra's success could pose to the status of their fiat money. The reason was that the dependence and trust in Libra, once entrenched in the ecosystem created by Facebook and other associated developers, would weaken the fiat money's dependency in their countries, a situation hated by the central banks wanting to dominate their currencies.

Institutions that had joined the Libra Association earlier quit one after another under the pressures of policies and regulations. They included PayPal, Visa, and Mastercard, payment giants in the U.S. Their departure undoubtedly dealt a heavy blow to Libra.

Some skeptics also criticized Libra for its risk of centralization due to their previous experience of Facebook's credibility crisis caused by its inadvertent leak of user information.

Beset with challenges at home and abroad, the scheduled 2020 launch of Libra hung in the balance. Interestingly, the mythology of the Greek Goddess of Justice holding the scales in her hand also has a tragic ending. After the Greek pantheon returned to Heaven disappointed at evil human deeds, only the goddess wouldn't tear herself away. She insisted on teaching humans to be good. She was heartbroken and left for the sky, eventually becoming the Libra constellation, regarded as a totem of justice with the stars forming the scales.

97 Central Bank Digital Currency

Central Bank Digital Currency usually appears in the abbreviated "CBDC."

A CBDC can be described as a digital form of a country's fiat money, a "digital version" of a sovereign currency issued by an official financial authority, usually a central bank.

The Bank of England first released a CBDC proposal. Subsequent reports showed that 70% of the world's central banks were following up. The reports came from the International Monetary Fund (IMF), the Bank for International Settlements (BIS), and the International Business Machines Corporation (IBM), which contributed most of the code to Hyperledger. China is also one of the active explorers of CBDC.

Starting its research in CBDC in 2014, China has had a considerable reserve of patents. The final design of a CBDC hasn't yet been determined. However, from some related information, it follows that blockchain will be one of its underlying technologies.

China's CBDC project is called DCEP (Digital Currency Electronic Payment), according to Mu Changchun, director of the Central Bank's Digital Currency Research Institute. It will be a "digital currency and electronic payment tool" with the same attributes as banknotes. It's digital in form only.

A near-future scenario of using DCEP is like this: You don't have to bind your money with any bank account as long as your friends have DCEP digital

wallets on their mobile phones. The transfer of funds is at the convenience of a mutual touch of your phones.

Did you realize that, like an encrypted asset such as Bitcoin, DCEP is also free from the control of the traditional bank account system because it's merely an encrypted string of characters?

One of the reasons why most worldwide central banks are stepping up their research on CBDC is that there is uncertainty about commercial banks or third-party financial payment institutions. If PayPal in the United States went bankrupt, the user's money in PayPal could only participate in a bankruptcy liquidation. The probability is undeniable despite its low rate of occurrence in a centralized society.

Since CBDC isn't decentralized, its promotion will help the central banks of all the countries protect their currency sovereignty and fiat money status. On the other hand, issuing banknotes and coins is extremely expensive, with tremendous costs accrued from anti-counterfeiting technologies and a multi-layered circulation system. Therefore, cash is gradually fading out of daily use.

However, you may wonder whether CBDC, once used universally, will increase the pressure on central banks to fight money laundering. Laundering paper money in the past was fairly costly despite some degree of anonymity. Then, you'll ask if CBDC makes digital currency laundering less expensive.

Mu Changchun said that digital wallets would be graded, and the funds in them would be limited to deal with the money laundering problem. For example, if you register for a wallet only with a mobile phone number, the permission level must be the lowest, which can only meet the daily micropayment needs. But if you upload your ID card, you can get a higher-level digital wallet.

98 Tokenization

Tokenization means the tokenization of assets. You may look around your room: You'll see everything shares one thing in common, that is, indivisibility, ranging from small objects such as a painting hanging on the wall and a gold coin kept in a safe to things as large as your house.

You can't ask for 1% of the real property rights if you want to buy a house. For that matter, you can't claim 1% of the ownership of *Starry Night*. But tokenization divides these indivisible assets into small units in the form of tokens as small as a figure far from the right of a decimal point.

Let's give free rein to our imagination together. Suppose a hyper-realistic painting worth 10 million yuan was tokenized into 10 million tokens. As an investor, can you claim 1% of the ownership of the artwork with 100,000 tokens?

However, you may be confused at this point, wondering if tokenization only digitizes assets unsophisticatedly. Don't forget the value provided by the underlying blockchain technology.

To be more accurate, you can treat the tokenized painting as a blockchain, and the cryptocurrency issued on the chain is the tokens in your hand. Every token transaction will be recorded in the public ledger, and no one can fabricate it. The flexibility and convenience of token transactions considerably facilitate liquidating the investment in this artwork.

However, such a scenario is still in the imagination. Fully tokenizing and "blockchainizing" real-world assets still face many challenges. For example, this tokenized painting doesn't belong to an individual or institution as one piece. Who will keep it in that case? How can I ensure that it is properly stowed in a physical space? Who will be accountable in the event of its being stolen? In the final analysis, how the physical properties of assets are genuinely reflected on the blockchain is still a problem that remains unsolved.

99 The Internet of Value

The birth of the Internet has ushered in an era of information explosion. When you share a song or post a selfie, you're sending a "message." The Internet allows "information" to disseminate by breaking through geographical barriers at a considerably low cost.

But such an "information-oriented" Internet is far from perfect. The biggest problem is that you can't be sure of the information's authenticity. In other words, you can never really "trust" what's circulated on it.

Because of that, strangers may be able to send information on a P2P network, but they can't transfer the value of the information in the same manner. In a beautifully imagined scenario about the Internet of Value, strangers can trade with each other trustfully without relying on any centralized third party, which can be a bank, a real estate agent, or an online car-hailing app, to transfer value. Such an era would be called the era of the Internet of Value.

If the trust issue isn't resolved, let's examine what would happen when you conduct a P2P transaction.

Someone wants to transfer 100 yuan to you on WeChat. From the perspective of digital code, he sends a "message" about the transfer to this social media. Behind the WeChat payment is the authoritative accounting system of financial institutions, recording the information of him transferring 100 yuan to you in the ledger. Then, that person can no longer claim that he

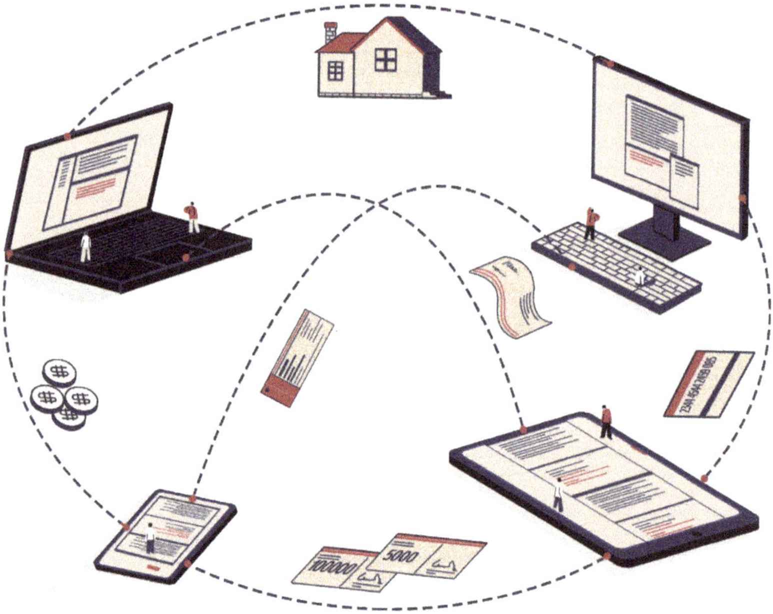

has remitted the same funds to others.

Now, let's get rid of this accounting system. Without a reliable bookkeeper, you won't know if he has sent the same "message" to someone else, and this "message" can be replicated indefinitely at no cost. So, you can't agree to a transaction on the Internet without worries.

Have you considered banking fees, online car-hailing platform commissions, or real estate agent commissions? We're paying a lot for such "trust" in the "information Internet" era.

Blockchain uses an immutable code system to lay the foundation of trust so that strangers can realize P2P value transfer through cryptocurrency. In an ideal ecosystem of the Internet of value, transaction costs will also become lower after eliminating the centralized third-party platform.

www.ingramcontent.com/pod-product-compliance
Lightning Source LLC
Chambersburg PA
CBHW041144230326
41599CB00039BA/7157